Generis
PUBLISHING

The Health Care Services Outreach in Microfinance Institutions

Van Duong Ha
Pham Trong Khang Ha

Title: The Health Care Services Outreach in Microfinance Institutions

ISBN: 979-8-89248-163-2

Author: Van Duong Ha, Pham Trong Khang Ha

Cover image: www.pixabay.com

Publisher: Generis Publishing
Online orders: www.generis-publishing.com
Contact email: info@generis-publishing.com

CONTENTS

RELATIONSHIP BETWEEN BED OCCUPANCY RATE AND AVERAGE DAYS PER INPATIENT 7

HEALTH CARE ACCESS AND HEALTH MANAGEMENT PERFORMANCE 29

THE INTERACTION RELATIONSHIP BETWEEN THE DIVERSIFICATION OF HEALTH CARE SUPPORT ACTIVITIES AND THE HEALTH CARE SERVICES OUTREACH IN MICROFINANCE INSTITUTIONS 52

RELATIONSHIP BETWEEN BED OCCUPANCY RATE AND AVERAGE DAYS PER INPATIENT

Pham Trong Khang Ha[1*], Van Duong Ha[2]
[1] Faculty of Medicine, University of Medicine Pham Ngoc Thach, Ho Chi Minh City, Vietnam.
[2] Saigon Institute of Economics and Technology, Ho Chi Minh City, Vietnam
E mail: [1] khangha.pt@gmail.com ; [2] dhv05@yahoo.com

Abstract

High bed occupancy rates have been considered an indicator of high hospital productivity, and average days per inpatient referred as an indicator of efficiency in healthcare service delivery. Reducing the bed occupancy rate contributes to ensure clinical safety, and reduction in the average days per inpatient can be a sign of good care coordination. The study aims is to examine relationship between bed occupancy rate and average days per inpatient. Using the time series data analytics in two models that factors affecting bed occupancy rate and factors affecting average days per inpatient, this study collected health data from the Ministry of health and General statistics office of Vietnam for the years 1990 - 2019. The results suggest a positive correlation between bed occupancy rate and average days per inpatient. While healthcare expenditures per total gross domestic product was negatively associated with average days per inpatient, and health budget per capita also was negatively associated with average days per inpatient. The study showed that an increase in average days per inpatient had a positive relationship with bed occupancy rate, doctors per 10,000 inhabitants was positive associated with bed occupancy rate, and pharmacists per 10000 inhabitants also had a positive relationship with bed occupancy rate. Base on this and prior research, policy implications include that investing and spending carefully in healthcare aspects would reduce average days per inpatient, and contribute to ensure clinically safe. These findings support arguments that high bed occupancy rate may also have implications for clinically and patient safety.

Keywords: Average days per inpatient, bed occupancy rate, healthcare, healthcare expenditures, health budget per capita.

1. INTRODUCTION

There is a link between bed occupancy rate and average days per inpatient that is an important consideration in healthcare. Many studies have found that improvements in bed occupancy rate can lead to an increase in average days per inpatient and vice versa. Bed occupancy rate holds a significant place in the productivity of hospital, and average days per inpatient refer as an indicator of efficiency in healthcare service delivery.

Vietnam's healthcare industry is growing fast, and thanks to the widespread coverage of Vietnam's grassroots health care system, health care services contributed to complete the millennium development goal relating health, and successfully controlled and eliminated many dangerous diseases. However, the health care services system still has a range of limitations at the grassroots level, such as low quality, the shortage of medical equipment and medicines, limited capacity of health workers, high bed occupancy rate, problems of overcrowding in the national level hospitals, implementing to lower the average days per inpatient further, among others. To prevent limitations at the grassroots level, the project on building and developing grassroots health care network has implemented in many years. This project focused on equipment, material facilities, financial supply, professional skills, human resources. At the same time, to prevent overcrowding in the national level hospitals, implementing to lower the average days per inpatient further, the government promulgate the investment incentive policies, many new hospitals and clinics have sprung up to cater to the patients.

There are many studies on the health care services system in Vietnam, but there are no studies on the relationship between bed occupancy rate and average days per inpatient in Vietnam. Addressing this gap, the study's purpose was to examine the factors affecting bed occupancy rate and factors affecting average days per inpatient. The study data will be collected from the Ministry of health and General statistics office of Vietnam for the years 1990 - 2019, and later on will be analyzed by statistical technique and tools, and applied a quantitative approach. This study has developed an in-depth analysis of the bed occupancy rate, the average days per inpatient, and found there was significant interaction between them on positive trends. These findings support arguments that high bed occupancy rate may also have implications for clinically and patient safety, and contribute to the theoretical and experimental on the health care services. Base on this and prior research, policy implications include that investing and spending carefully in healthcare aspects would reduce average days per inpatient, and contribute to ensure clinically safe, and further emphasizes optimal policies to healthcare aspects management. Investing and spending in human resource, science, technology in healthcare aspects is something that needs rational distribution further. Therefore, this study is urgently required to understand the factors affecting bed occupancy rate and factors affecting average days per inpatient. In particular, this has created an opportunity for the hospitals to tackle one of the biggest barriers to many requirements to ensure clinically safe.

2. LITERATURE REVIEW

2.1. Bed Occupancy Rate

There are many definitions of bed occupancy rate, and there is no agreed definition for the bed occupancy rate. Bed occupancy rate was defined as the number of occupied beds divided by the number of available staffed beds, times 100. It was possible to calculate the daily bed occupancy rate for specialty and hospital (Baillie et al., 1997). The bed occupancy rate was calculated from beds occupied at midnight compared with the total acute bed stock, including specialist beds (Cooke, Wilson, Halsall, & Roalfe, 2004). Bed occupancy rate was measured as the number of patients per available beds (Weissman et al., 2007). Theb ed occupancy rate considers as a measure of the ability of a hospital to function safely and effectively. High bed occupancy rate reflects clinically unsafe (Keegan, 2010). The bed occupancy rate had been considered an indicator of productivity for hospitals. The number of patients assigned to a department were divided the number of staffed beds in this department that was a bed occupancy rate (Madsen, Ladelund, & Linneberg, 2014). The bed occupancy rate was defined as the number of occupied medical beds divided by the total bed base at hospital (Boden et al., 2016). The bed occupancy rate was a measure of utilization of the available bed capacity. It reflected the percentage of beds occupied by inpatients in a defined period of time (Sindhu, Reddy, Satyanarayana, Devaraya, & Fathima, 2019). Therefore, bed occupancy rate is a measure that reflects the functional ability of a hospital. It is a calculation, which is used to measure the percentage of beds that are occupied by inpatients in relation to the total number of beds for a given time period. Bed occupancy is a quantitative indicator and it is influenced by many factors, including average days per inpatient, doctor per 10,000 inhabitants, growth rate of insured people, pharmacists per 10000 inhabitants, number of consultations.

Firstly, average days per inpatient: The average days per inpatient was often used as an indicator of efficiency, and referred to the average number of days that patients stayed in hospital. A high bed occupancy rate might not necessarily be running effectively. This could be due to the high average number of days that patients spent in hospital. Because, the numbers of patients being treated that had the longer lengths of stay in hospital (Baillie et al., 1997). The implications of high bed occupancy rate reflected relatively efficient situations, as the patients with many lengths of stay in hospital (Salah, Walsh, & Nandakumar, 1997). In the research of hospital performance assessment found that there was an inverse relationship between average days per inpatient and bed occupancy rate (Nwagbara, Rasiah, & Aslam, 2016).

Hypothesis 1.1 (H1.1): Average days per inpatient has positive or negative effect on bed occupancy rate.

Secondly, doctors per 10,000 inhabitants: A research found that the doctors per 10,000 inhabitants continues to increase, but the nember of doctors were not equally distributed in the healthcare system. At the same time, the number of inpatient beds continued to decline, and bed occupancy rate remained high (NCHS, 2010). An increase in doctors per 10,000 inhabitants was considered as an adequate supply of doctors was necessary to provide quality health care, and this contributed to increase the bed occupancy rates (NCHS, 2017). Bed occupancy rate cannot be defined without taking into account healthcare needs, staffing patterns, and other relevant aspects. This showed the doctors per 10,000 inhabitants was one of the factors that associated to define a bed occupancy rate rate (Ravaghi, Alidoost, Mannion, & Bélorgeot, 2020).

Hypothesis 1.2 (H1.2): Doctors per 10,000 inhabitants has a positive effect on bed occupancy rate.

Thirdly, growth rate of insured people: The rapid increase in health insurance coverage led to improve the growth rate of insured people, and were associated with a jump in hospital admissions. Thereby this contributed to increase the bed occupancy rate in the hospitals (Barber, Borowitz, Bekedam, & Ma, 2014). A growth rate of insured people was one of the factors affected the length of stay in hospital, thereby it had a positive impact on the bed occupancy rate (Ravaghi et al., 2020).

Hypothesis 1.3 (H1.3): Growth rate of insured people has a positive effect on bed occupancy rate.

Fourthly, pharmacists per 10,000 inhabitants: The resources in the health sector included doctors and pharmacists that contributed to increase bed occupancy rate. Therefore the pharmacists per 10000 inhabitants had a positive impact on the bed occupacy rate (Lieberman & Wagstaff, 2009). The bed occupancy rate of above 85 percent considered to have bed shortages, and the resources should be allocated were the causes and effects of bed shortages (Madsen et al., 2014). This showed the human resources such as doctors and pharmacists associated with bed occupancy rate, thereby the pharmacists per 10,000 inhabitants was one of the factors impact on the bed occupancy rate.

Hypothesis 1.4 (H1.4): Pharmacists per 10,000 inhabitants has a positive effect on bed occupancy rate.

Fifthly, number of consultations: The number of consultations referred to patients accepted for inpatient services in the hospitals within the same period. In the research of hospital performance assessment found that there was a positive relationship between number of consultations and bed occupancy rate (Nwagbara et al., 2016). An increase in bed occupancy rate was associated with a rise in the discharge rate, the readmission rate for discharged patients, and these showed the number of consultations was associated with the bed occupancy rates. In particular, these became more pronounced as high bed occupancy rate (Friebel et al., 2019).

Hypothesis 1.5 (H1.5): Number of consultations has a positive effect on bed occupancy rate.

2.2. Average Days Per Inpatient

The average days per inpatient measured the average days of stay in the hospital per admitted patient (Qureshi & Hassan, 2014). The average days per inpatient was an indicator which measured the average duration of hospital stay of admitted patients (Usman, Memon, & Shaikh, 2015). The average days per inpatient referred to the average number of days that patient's stayed in the hospital. It was calculated by dividing the total number of days spent in the hospital by the number of admissions or discharges in the same period (Aurthi & Rahaman, 2017). The average days per inpatient referred to the average number of days that patients stayed in hospital. The total number of days spent by all inpatients during a year were divided the number of admissions or discharges that were the average days per inpatient (OECD, 2017). The average days per inpatient was calculated by dividing the total patient days during the given period by the number of discharges during that period (Sindhu et al., 2019). Therefore, there are many definitions of average days per inpatient, and is influenced to varying degrees by various other factors, such as bed occupancy rate, growth rate of insured people, health budget per capita, healthcare expenditures per total GDP and number of consultations.

Firstly, bed occupancy rate: Increased bed occupancy rate was strongly associated with the length of stay for admitted patients, and this contributed to increase the average days per inpatien (Forster, Stiell, Wells, Lee, & Van Walraven, 2003). High bed occupancy rates have been considered an indicator of high hospital productivity, associated with increased inpatient, caused bed shortages, and increased average days per inpatien (Madsen et al., 2014). The study data suggested that in terms of bed occupancy rate were found to run in optimal capacity which, but the average length of stay of patients reflect to be relatively longer which showed the bed occupancy rate had a positive relationship with average days per inpatien (Usman et al., 2015). While increased bed occupancy rate was associated with the average days per inpatient, this was more pronounced in older and sicker patients, and increased the average days per inpatient (Friebel et al., 2019).

Hypothesis 2.1 (H2.1): Bed occupancy rate has a positive effect on average days per inpatient.

Secondly, growth rate of insured people: The demand for the healthcare services has increased with increasing in the health insurance programs. The people used health insurance that were more likely to spend more days in inpatient treatment. This suggested that the growth rate of insured people might lead to an increase in the average days per inpatient (Tian, Tien, Chen, & Liu, 2012). The increase in health insurance coverage may lead to increase in healthcare services. The insured patients remained in the hospital longer, and insurance status strongly associates with days in inpatient treatment. This also showed that the growth rate of insured people might lead to an increase in the average days per inpatient (Englum et al., 2016). Average days per inpatient was another key factor for resource utilization and bed efficiency in the hospitals. Average days per inpatient was affected by a number of factors, such as patient characteristics and growth rate of insured people (Ravaghi et al., 2020).

Hypothesis 2.2 (H2.2): Growth rate of insured people has a positive effect on average days per inpatient.

Thirdly, health budget per capita: The length of stay would be reduce in the hospitals as the total health expenditures for the inpatients decreased in the healthcare system. This indicated health budget per capita had a positive relationship with the average days per inpatient (Fukawa & Izumida, 2004). Average days per inpatient might impact on a hospital functions from hight bed occupancy rate, and this might lead to additional costs and health budget per capita (Ravaghi et al., 2020). The average length of stay had decreased in hospitals and this decline was offset by an increase in healthcare costs per patient. Accordingly, an increase in health budget per capita could lead to reduce the average days per inpatient (Zhao et al., 2020).

Hypothesis 2.3 (H2.3): Health budget per capita has a positive or negative effect on average days per inpatient.

Fourthly, healthcare expenditures per total gross domestic product (GDP): There was an inverse relationship between the cost of healthcare and the average hospital stay; thereby, this could indicate healthcare expenditures per total GDP had a negative impact on the average days per inpatient (Puozaa, 2016). Healthcare expenditures was related to average hospital stay, reducing healthcare expenditures could create benefits and reduce average hospital stay. Thereby, this could show that reducing healthcare expenditures per total GDP contribute to decrease the average days per inpatient (Soong, Gillam, Bornstein, & Navarro, 2017). Any projections regarding hospital expenditures should also determine to wider healthcare system changes such as changes in average length of stay, and healthcare expenditures per total GDP (Ravaghi et al., 2020).

Hypothesis 2.4 (H2.4): Healthcare expenditures per total GDP has a positive or negative effect on average days per inpatient.

Fifthly, number of consultations: Optimising of average days per inpatient was one approach to improving clinical performance, and the admissions were associated with increased length of stay at the hospital level. In other words, the number of consultations were associated with average days per inpatient (Earnest, Chen, & Seow, 2006). The admission mode was associated with length of stay, and admission was associated with longer length of stay (Casalino et al., 2019). Infants and the elderly had the highest number of consultations, and hospital admission associated with many factors, particularly for length of stay (Zhao et al., 2020). Average days per inpatient was another key factor for resource utilization, and it was affected by a number of factors, such as time for conducting consultation services and number of consultations (Ravaghi et al., 2020).

Hypothesis 2.5 (H2.5): Number of consultations has a positive effect on average days per inpatient.

This study formulates the following hypotheses that focus on the two models that factors affecting bed occupancy rate and factors affecting average days per inpatient as can be seen in Figure 1.

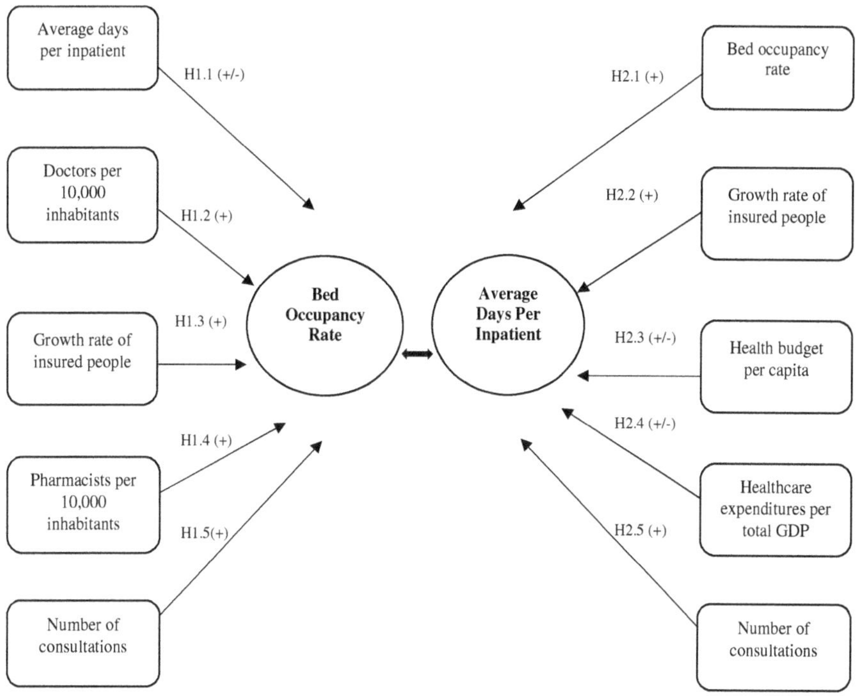

Figure 1. The relationships of the hypotheses

3. METHODS

This study collected health data from Vietnam health statistics yearbook of the Ministry of health and the statistical yearbook of General statistics office of Vietnam in the period of 1990 - 2019. The analysis models of factors affecting bed occupancy rate and factors affecting average days per inpatient were established as follows:

$$Y_1 = \alpha_{10} + \alpha_{11}Y_2 + \sum_{k=1}^{n} \beta_{1k}X_{1k} + \mu_1 \qquad (1)$$

$$Y_2 = \alpha_{20} + \alpha_{21}Y_1 + \sum_{\gamma=1}^{m} \beta_{2\gamma}X_{2\gamma} + \mu_2 \qquad (2)$$

Where,

Y_1 is a variable that measures bed occupancy rate, determined by the percentage of beds that are occupied by inpatients in relation to the total number of beds for a given time period. Y_2 is a variable that measures average days per inpatient, determined by the average days of stay in the hospital per admitted patient. X_{1k}, and $X_{2\gamma}$ are the independent variables that can affect bed occupancy rate and average days per inpatient in Equation 1 and Equation 2, respectively.The coefficient α and coefficient β are the correlation coefficients, and μ is the regression residual. For simplicity, indicator *i* shows the number of observations and indicator *t* shows the number observed year. This study used Stata 15.0 software with the variables described briefly and the definitions of the variables and their expected signs as shown in Table 1.

Table 1. *Summary of the research model variables*

Variables and symbols	Definition	Expected sign and hypotheses
Factors affecting bed occupancy rate		
Dependent variable		
Bed occupancy rate (BOR)	(Daily average of beds occupied / Bed complement) x 100	
Independent variables		
Average days per inpatient (ADI)	Total Patient days during the given period / Number of discharges during that period	H1.1: +/- (high AID, high or low BOR)
Doctors per 10,000 inhabitants (DPI)	Total doctors / 10,000 inhabitants	H1.2: + (high DPI, high BOR)
Growth rate of insured people (GIP)	Growth in number of insured people	H1.3: + (high GIP, high BOR)
Pharmacists per 10,000 inhabitants (PPI)	Total Pharmacists / 10,000 inhabitants	H1.4: + (high PPI, high BOR)
Number of consultations (NOC)	The number of contacts with physicians	H1.5: + (high NOC, high BOR)
Factors affecting average days per inpatient		
Dependent variable		
Average days per inpatient (ADI)	Total Patient days during the given period / Number of discharges during that period	
Independent variable		
Bed occupancy rate (BOR)	(Daily average of beds occupied / Bed complement) x 100	H2.1: + (high BOR, high ADI)
Growth rate of insured people (GIP)	Growth in number of insured people	H2.2: + (high GIP, high ADI)
Health budget per capita (HBC)	Health budget / Population	H2.3: +/- (high HBC, high or low ADI)
Healthcare expenditures per total GDP (HEG)	Healthcare expenditures / Total GDP	H2.4: +/- (high HEG, high or low ADI)
Number of consultations (NOC)	The number of contacts with physicians	H2.5: + (high NOC, high ADI)

This study applied multivariate regression, analyzed, evaluated the fluctuations of variables and performed the correlation analysis in the models. Finding correlation coefficients was carried out on each variable of the models. The multicollinearity tests, checking residual variance change, and the tests for auto-correlation were conducted in this research models.

4. RESULTS

4.1. Descriptive Statistics

The descriptive statistics results found that the ADI, BOR, DPI, HBC HEG, NOC and PPI variables had smaller standard deviations than the average, this showes that the values tend to be close to the mean of the variables. The healthcare system in Vietnam has gradually decreased the average days per inpatient over the years, and this indicator had the lowest point of 1.39 and the highest was 7.35. The bed occupancy rate had gradually decreased over the years, and it had the lowest was 128.97 and the highest achieveed 102.17. The annual increase in the number of trained doctors and pharmacists have added to the human resources of hospitals and contributed to increase the doctors per 10,000 inhabitants; and these indicators obtained 6.32 of the lowest and the highest attained 8.8 for the doctors per 10,000 inhabitants, and the lowest was 1.19 and the highest was 2.96 for the pharmacists per 10,000 inhabitants. The health expenditures included healthcare goods and services consumed and increased during each year. This contributed to increase the health budget per capita and the healthcare expenditures per total GDP. The healthcare system in Vietnam consists primarily of hospitals and commune health stations; besides there is more and more quality hospitals built and operated in the country, and This contributed to increase the number of consultations over the years. The growth rate of insured people had fluctuations, this indicates that the values are spread out over a wider range, as the number of insured people changed rapidly from 2009 to 2019.

Table 2 *Descriptive statistics*

Variable	Mean	Std. Dev.	Min	Max
ADI	6.107143	2.012237	1.39	7.35
BOR	113.6643	7.88817	102.17	128.97
DPI	7.549286	.8566434	6.23	8.8
GIP	.0654541	.0858776	.0046359	.3448276
HBC	1379.357	763.3927	586.5	2951
HEG	3.444286	.4295027	2.63	4.02
NOC	208204.4	8301.532	196456.6	229775.7
PPI	2.132857	.6202658	1.19	2.96

Source: Authors' calculation from Stata 15.0.

4.2. Correlation Analysis

The analysis results of correlation between variables was smaller than .70 (-.70). These results showed that the degree of correlation between the variables from negligible correlation to the moderate correlation. Because, the size of a correlation coefficient showed that moderate positive (negative) correlation with size of correlation from .50 to .70 (−.50 to −.70); low positive (negative) correlation with size of correlation from .30 to .50 (−.30 to −.50); negligible correlation with size of correlation from .00 to .30 (.00 to −.30) (Hinkle, Wiersma, & Jurs, 2003). So, the presence of any multicollinearity was neglected in the models, as can be seen in Table 3.

Table 3. *Correlation matrix*

Correlation matrix for factors affecting bed occupancy rate

	BOR	ADI	DPI	GIP	NOC	PPI
BOR	1.0000					
ADI	0.5453	1.0000				
DPI	0.0619	-0.5899	1.0000			
GIP	0.2089	0.2082	-0.1513	1.0000		
NOC	0.1609	-0.0438	0.5215	0.0547	1.0000	
PPI	0.0106	-0.5512	0.6503	0.0328	0.6270	1.0000

Correlation matrix for factors affecting average days per inpatient

	ADI	BOR	GIP	HBC	HEG	NOC
ADI	1.0000					
BOR	0.5453	1.0000				
GIP	0.2082	0.2089	1.0000			
HBC	-0.5329	-0.1871	-0.1473	1.0000		
HEG	-0.5305	-0.0217	0.2572	0.5447	1.0000	
NOC	-0.0438	0.1609	0.0547	0.5230	0.5008	1.0000

Source: Authors' calculation from Stata 15.0.

4.3. Regression Results

In the model of factors affecting bed occupancy rate showed the variables ADI, DPI and PPI had positive impacts on the variable BOR at the significance level of 5%, 10% and 10%, respectively. The variable GIP had a positive impact on the variable BOR, and the variable NOC had a negative impact on the variable BOR, but these variables were not statistically significant in this mode as can be seen in Table 4. The study examined multicollinearity for factors affecting BOR had a result of Mean VIF = 1.38, VIF of variables from 1.06 to 1.72, this indicated no serious multicollinearity in this model. Checking residual variance change with P-value = 0.3738 was greater than 0.05, therefore, there was not the variance change phenomenon in this model.

Table 4. *Regression results for factors affecting bed occupancy rate*

Independent variables	Dependent variable (BOR)
ADI	3.849**
	(3.78)
DPI	3.543*
	(3.23)
GIP	0.106
	(0.01)
NOC	-1.761
	(0.402)
PPI	0.013*
	(2.53)
_cons	90.61
	(0.034)

Notes: ***, **, * denote significance at the level of 1%, 5% and 10%
Source: Compiled from data processing results of Stata software

In the model of factors affecting average days per inpatient found the variable BOR had positive relationship with the variable ADI at the significance level of 10%. The variables HBC, and HEG had negative relationships with the variable ADI at the significance level of 10% and 1%, respectively. The variables GIP, and NOC had positive relationships with the variable ADI, but these variables were not statistically significant in this mode as can be seen in Table 5. The study examined multicollinearity for factors affecting ADI had a result of Mean VIF = 2.21, VIF of variables from 1.18 to 3.51, this indicated no serious multicollinearity in this model. Checking residual variance change with P-value = 0.4421 was greater than 0.05, therefore, there was not the variance change phenomenon in this model.

Table 5. *Regression results for factors affecting average days per inpatient*

Independent variables	Dependent variable (ADI)
BOR	0.107*
	(3.09)
GIP	0.942
	(0.75)
HBC	-0.00165*
	(-3.80)
HEG	-0.806***
	(-5.51)
NOC	7.642
	(2.11)
_cons	-16.96
	(0.048)

Notes: ***, **, * denote significance at the level of 1%, 5% and 10%
Source: Compiled from data processing results of Stata software

5. DISCUSSIONS

The results in Table 4 showed that variable ADI had a positive impact on the variable BOR with coefficient 3.849, and with the significance level of 5%, indicating that average days per inpatient had a strong impact on bed occupancy rate. This result showed that for one unit increased in the average days per inpatient, the bed occupancy rate was anticipated to increase by 3.849 units, when the remaining variables in the model were kept constant. This result agreed with the analysis results of Baillie et al. (1997) and Salah et al. (1997), and disagreed with the findings of Nwagbara, et al. (2016). Overcrowding in hospitals was one of the problems that the healthcare sector have been dealing with. This was due to the high average number of days that patients spent in the hospitals, the numbers of patients being treated that had the longer lengths of stay in hospital; so, a high bed occupancy rate might not necessarily be running effectively. The healthcare system in Vietnam has a sizeable number of hospitals across the country. As of figures from 2019, there were over 13,550 health facilities, in branch, provincial, and national levels. However, 75% of them were built more than 22 years ago, and shortage of medical staff and obsolete equipments, and intensive care units werw also some problems that the healthcare sector have been dealing with. On the other hand, the quality and availability of healthcare services were critical components for many patients, and they spent more time searching the hospitals in major cities, which has led to overcrowd in these hospitals.

The outcome of the regression analysis indicated the variable DPI had a coefficient 3.543 with the significance level of 10%. This showed that increasing the doctors per 10,000 inhabitants improved the bed occupancy rate by 3.543 units per year. As expected, this result was broadly in harmony with the expected sign and hypotheses, and agreed with the study of NCHS (2010), NCHS (2017), and Ravaghi et al.(2020). There was a complement relationship exists between the doctors per 10,000 inhabitants and the bed occupancy rate. The quality of healthcare services, professional medical skills and a team of excellent doctors were critical components for many patients. While, shortage of docrors was one of the problems that the healthcare system have been dealing with. So, the patients spent more time searching the national-level hospitals in the city than to a smaller hospital within their province as they feel the quality of care would be much better. This showed that patients' perception of health care quality in small provincial HCPs is still questioned in Vietnam. Thereby, an increase in doctors per 10,000 inhabitants was considered as an adequate supply of doctors was necessary to provide quality health care, and this contributed to increase the bed occupancy rates over the years in the healthcare system.

The outcome of the regression analysis indicated there was a statistically significant effect of the pharmacists per 10,000 inhabitants on the bed occupancy rate. As expected, the study noted a coefficient that was significant at the 10% level. This result showed that for one unit increase in the pharmacists per 10,000 inhabitants, the bed occupancy rate was anticipated to increase by 0.013 units, when the remaining variables in the model were kept constant. As expected, this result was broadly in harmony with the expected sign and hypotheses, and agreed with the study of Lieberman and Wagstaff (2009), and Madsen et al. (2014). Other factors affecting the patients' perception of health care quality were the shortage of shortages of medicines and medical equipments for critical care, as well as the wide availability of pharmacies. Many people were in the long lines at the overcrowded hospitals, especially in public hospitals where they wait to get medicine to treat patients in hospital due to shortage of medical staff. With a shortage of human resource such as doctors, nurses and pharmacists tending to the huge number of patients every day, the healthcare service system requires a huge, well-trained workforce, and the pharmacists resources were allocated that contributed to increase the pharmacists per 10,000 inhabitants, while the healthcare system in Vietnam was facing overcrowding in hospitals problems too.

The results in Table 5 indicated that variable BOR had a positive relationship with the variable ADI with coefficient 0.107, and with the significance level of 10%. This result showed that for one unit increased in the bed occupancy rate, the average days per inpatient was anticipated to increase by 0.107 units, when the remaining variables in the model were kept constant. As expected, this result was broadly in harmony with the expected sign and hypotheses, and agreed with the findings of Forster et al. (2003), Madsen et al. (2014), Usman et al. (2015), and Friebel et al. (2019). Overcrowding in hospitals led to an increase in the bed occupancy rate, and this resulted from an increased patient, many patients have to wait in a hallway for days before a bed becomes available. The bed occupancy rate of above 85 percent was generally reflectred to have bed shortages (Madsen et al., 2014); this rate is always 100 percent higher in the healthcare system, especially at the provincial and city levels in Vietnam. The bed occupancy rate started increasing from 1991 onward, and high bed occupancy rate might affect the healthcare quality, and might lead to a risk for patient. The average days per inpatient were relatively longer, especially for patients affected byhospital-associated infections, the length of stay is very long.

The model result exhibited a significant effect of the health budget per capita on the average days per inpatient, and the coefficient was negative and statistically significant at the 10% level. This result showed that for one unit reduce in the health budget per capita, the average days per inpatient was anticipated to increase by 0.00165 units, when the remaining variables in the model were kept constant. This result was broadly in harmony with the study of Zhao et al. (2020), and disagreed with the findings of Fukawa and Izumida (2004) and Ravaghi et al. (2020). This showed that average days per inpatient might not result simply from a bed occupancy rate and bed shortages but might also involve the health budget per capita. Overcrowding in hospitals results in a strain on the infrastructure of healthcare facilities. To prevent overcrowding in hospitals, the government continued to finance the investment of new hospitals. For the public hospitals in Vietnam relied largely on a state budget to maintain and upgrade the facilities as most of them were invest more than two decades ago and need to be upgraded. The budget has increased in over the years, it contributed to increase health budget per capita per capita, and the health budget was close to USD130 per capita in 2019. Accordingly, the increased health budget per capita per capita increased the productivity, and reduced average days per inpatient.

The regression result indicated a very significant effect of the healthcare expenditures per total GDP on the average days per inpatient, and the coefficient was negative and statistically significant at the 1% level. This result showed that for one unit reduce in the healthcare expenditures per total GDP, the average days per inpatient was anticipated to increase by 0.806 units, when the remaining variables in the model were kept constant. This result agreed with the study of Puozaa (2016), and was not broadly in harmony with the study of Soong et al. (2017), and Ravaghi et al. (2020). This also showed that average days per inpatient might not result simply from a bed occupancy rate, bed shortages, and the health budget per capita but might also involve the healthcare expenditures per total GDP. The healthcare expenditure in Vietnam increased every year and by 2019, healthcare expenditure accounted more than 5% of the gross domestic product, and the health budget was close to USD130 per capita in 2019. Healthcare expenditure was a way that can result in better provision of health opportunities, secure the resources needed to diagnose and treat patients, which contributed to reduce the average days per inpatien.

6. CONCLUSIONS AND RECOMMENDATIONS

The bed occupancy rate and average days per inpatient have been considered an indicator of hospital productivity. Reducing the bed occupancy rate contributes to ensure clinical safety, and reduction in the average days per inpatient can be a sign of good care coordination. This paper studied relationship between bed occupancy rate and average days per inpatient of the healthcare system in Vietnam. Multiple regression analysis was applied in this study to find out the potential factors that affect bed occupancy rate and average days per inpatient. Based on previous research, two prominent models have been identified and these research results were accurate according to the characteristics, and the development history of the healthcare system in Vietnam from 1990 to 2019.

The study results showed that the three factors that had positive relationships with the bed occupancy rate were the average days per inpatient, doctors per 10,000 inhabitants, and pharmacists per 10000 inhabitants. This study also showed that one factor that had a positive relationship with the average days per inpatient was the bed occupancy rate. The health budget per capita and the healthcare expenditures per total GDP had negative relationships with the average days per inpatient. This study can conclude that two dependence variables of the two models were statistically significant, and there was relationship between bed occupancy rate and average days per inpatient in a positive trend.

Nowadays, the healthcare are having a significant investment prospects in many regions of the country. This study helps the researchers, investors, and managers develop their expertise in the key determinants of the bed occupancy rate and average days per inpatient, and the relationships between bed occupancy rate and average days per inpatient. Based on the research results, the article recommends the following to reduce bed occupancy rate and average days per inpatient.

Firstly, the influence of bed occupancy rate on the average days per inpatient has been recognized from the study results. the healthcare system included the commune level, district level, provincial level and national level facilities, provides the country with a high average days per inpatient, and it still has not solved the issues of high bed occupancy rate and the healthcare system continues to far exceed the 80 percent bed occupancy rate. Therefore, hospitals should realize that increasing bed occupancy rate will not solve the problem of hospital overcrowding. On the other hand, bed occupancy rate has increased to levels considered clinically unsafe. This high rate might lead to the possibility of adverse events as it has been related to an increased likelihood of infections and unsafe patients. Thus, the hospitals need focuses on determining the optimal number of beds to allocate to each their unit. Moreover, The hospials should consider alternative approaches to planning hospital capacity to fix the limitations of bed occupancy rate.

Secondly, the average days per inpatient was shortened that creates many advantages. The patients spend less time in hospital, it helps them more safety and leads to less consumption of drugs. Accordingly, the hospitals reduce the bed occupancy rate and overcrowding in hospitals, restrict to use many resources, and the healthcare system will improve the operations. Therefore, the healthcare system should stress the significance of renovation of the health system in Vietnam, perform the efficient exploitation of all resources, use all resources to the fullest potential. Thereby, it helps the country achieve the target of universal health care coverage.

Thirdly, in order to modernize the healthcare system will require heavy investment and the government will continue to finance the construction of new hospitals. At the same time, the governmentcontinues to strengthen policies to encourage investment in hospitals, especially attracting investment from various sources of investment to upgrade, and build its medical facilities. These contribute to an increase in the healthcare expenditures per total GDP, and contribute to reducing overcrowding in hospitals and the average days per inpatient.

Fourthly, investing and spending in human resource, science, technology in healthcare aspects is something that concentrates rational distribution further. The hospitals should increase to invest new technologies that help them possible for complex interventions to be undertaken in inpatient treatment. With modern diagnostic and therapeutic equipment and new interventional medical procedures will contribute to faster and more efficient treatment. Thereby, reducing the average days per inpatient will increase the turnover rate, and reduce bed occupancy rate that would enable a greater number of patients to benefit from treatment.

References

Aurthi, A. Y., & Rahaman, A. (2017). Average Length of Stay (ALS) of under Five Years Hospitalized Children: A Study on Bangladesh. *J Heal Scien, 7*(5), 96-100.

Baillie, H., Wright, W., McLeod, A., Craig, N., Leyland, A., Drummond, N., & Boddy, A. (1997). *Bed occupancy and bed management.* University of Glasgow: Public Health Research Unit.

Barber, S. L., Borowitz, M., Bekedam, H., & Ma, J. (2014). The hospital of the future in China: China's reform of public hospitals and trends from industrialized countries. *Health policy and planning, 29*(3), 367-378.

Boden, D., Agarwal, A., Hussain, T., Martin, S., Radford, N., Riyat, M., . . . Whale, C. (2016). Lowering levels of bed occupancy is associated with decreased inhospital mortality and improved performance on the 4-hour target in a UK District General Hospital. *Emergency Medicine Journal, 33*(2), 85-90.

Casalino, E., Perozziello, A., Choquet, C., Curac, S., Leroy, C., & Hellmann, R. (2019). Evaluation of hospital length of stay and revenues as a function of admission mode, clinical pathways including observation unit stay and hospitalization characteristics. *Health services management research, 32*(1), 16-25.

Cooke, M., Wilson, S., Halsall, J., & Roalfe, A. (2004). Total time in English accident and emergency departments is related to bed occupancy. *Emergency Medicine Journal, 21*(5), 575-576.

Earnest, A., Chen, M. I., & Seow, E. (2006). Exploring if day and time of admission is associated with average length of stay among inpatients from a tertiary hospital in Singapore: an analytic study based on routine admission data. *BMC Health Services Research, 6*(1), 1-8.

Englum, B. R., Hui, X., Zogg, C. K., Chaudhary, M. A., Villegas, C., Bolorunduro, O. B., . . . Efron, D. T. (2016). Association between insurance status and hospital length of stay following trauma. *The American Surgeon, 82*(3), 281-288.

Forster, A. J., Stiell, I., Wells, G., Lee, A. J., & Van Walraven, C. (2003). The effect of hospital occupancy on emergency department length of stay and patient disposition. *Academic Emergency Medicine, 10*(2), 127-133.

Friebel, R., Fisher, R., Deeny, S. R., Gardner, T., Molloy, A., & Steventon, A. (2019). The implications of high bed occupancy rates on readmission rates in England: A longitudinal study. *Health Policy, 123*(8), 765-772.

Fukawa, T., & Izumida, N. (2004). Japanese healthcare expenditures in a comparative context. *The Japanese journal of social security policy, 3*(2), 51-61.

Hinkle, D. E., Wiersma, W., & Jurs, S. G. (2003). *Applied statistics for the behavioral sciences* (Vol. 663): Houghton Mifflin College Division.

Keegan, A. D. (2010). Hospital bed occupancy: more than queuing for a bed. *Medical Journal of Australia, 193*(5), 291-293.

Lieberman, S. S., & Wagstaff, A. (2009). *Health financing and delivery in Vietnam: looking forward*: World Bank Publications.

Madsen, F., Ladelund, S., & Linneberg, A. (2014). High levels of bed occupancy associated with increased inpatient and thirty-day hospital mortality in Denmark. *Health Affairs, 33*(7), 1236-1244.

NCHS. (2010). *Health, United States, 2009 With special feature on medical technology*. Washington, DC: US Department of Health and Human Services, Centers for Disease Control, National Center for Health Statistics.

NCHS. (2017). *Health, United States, 2016: With Chartbook on Long-term Trends in Health*. Washington, DC: Government Printing Office.

Nwagbara, V., Rasiah, R., & Aslam, M. (2016). An approach toward public hospital performance assessment. *Medicine, 95*(36), e4688-e4688.

OECD. (2017). Average length of stay in hospitals. In *Health at a Glance 2017: OECD Indicators*. Paris: OECD Publishing.

Puozaa, C. Y. (2016). The determinants of hospital length of stay in Nigeria. *International Journal of Business and Economic Sciences Applied Research (IJBESAR), 9*(3), 34-42.

Qureshi, W., & Hassan, G. (2014). A five year retrospective study of bed utilization trends in a tertiary care teaching institution. *JK Science, 16*(3), 119 -121.

Ravaghi, H., Alidoost, S., Mannion, R., & Bélorgeot, V. D. (2020). Models and methods for determining the optimal number of beds in hospitals and regions: a systematic scoping review. *BMC Health Services Research, 20*(1), 1-13.

Salah, H., Walsh, J., & Nandakumar, A. (1997). *Cost Analysis and Efficiency Indicators for Health Care*. Retrieved from https://cdn1.sph.harvard.edu/wp-content/uploads/sites/1989/2020/01/Egypt_No-56_.pdf

Sindhu, J., Reddy, K., Satyanarayana, N., Devaraya, S., & Fathima, A. (2019). Hospital Utilizationn Statistics: Thirty-Five Year Trend Analysis, A Measure of Operational Efficiency of a Tertiary Care Teaching Institute in South India. *IOSR J Dent Med Sci, 18*(4), 49-55.

Soong, C., Gillam, S., Bornstein, S., & Navarro, P. (2017). *Reducing Acute Care Length of Stay in Newfoundland & Labrador*. St. John's, NL: Newfoundland & Labrador Centre for Applied Health Research. Memorial University.

Tian, W.-H., Tien, J. J., Chen, C.-S., & Liu, T.-C. (2012). Private Health Insurance and Inpatient Service Utilisation among Adults and Elderly People under Taiwan's National Insurance Programme. *Geneva Papers on Risk and Insurance. Issues and Practice*, 655-677.

Usman, G., Memon, K. N., & Shaikh, S. (2015). Bed occupancy rate and length of stay of patients in Medical and allied wards of a tertiary care hospital. *Journal of Ayub Medical College Abbottabad, 27*(2), 367-370.

Weissman, J. S., Rothschild, J. M., Bendavid, E., Sprivulis, P., Cook, E. F., Evans, R. S., . . . Haug, P. (2007). Hospital workload and adverse events. *Medical care*, 448-455.

Zhao, Q., Coelho, M. S., Li, S., Saldiva, P. H., Abramson, M. J., Huxley, R. R., & Guo, Y. (2020). Trends in hospital admission rates and associated direct healthcare costs in Brazil: a nationwide retrospective study between 2000 and 2015. *Innovation, 38*(30), 1-30.

HEALTH CARE ACCESS AND HEALTH MANAGEMENT PERFORMANCE

Pham Trong Khang Ha[1*], Van Duong Ha[2]

[1] Faculty of Medicine, University of Medicine Pham Ngoc Thach, Ho Chi Minh City, Vietnam.

[2] Saigon Institute of Economics and Technology, Ho Chi Minh City, Vietnam

E mail: [1] khangha.pt@gmail.com ; [2] dhv05@yahoo.com

Abstract

Increasing in the health care access is one of the goals towards universal health coverage; the health management performance is considered an indicator of efficiency in healthcare service delivery that is represented as average days per inpatient. Increasing in the health care access contributes to advance the ability of healthcare services in the prevention, diagnosis, treatment, and management of diseases; at the same time, reducing the average days per inpatient may be an indication of good care coordination. The study aims is to examine relationship between health care access and health management performance. This study used the time series data analytics in two models that factors affecting health care access and health management performance. The health data is collected from the Ministry of health and General statistics office of Vietnam for the years 1990 - 2019. The study showed that an increase in the health management performance had a negative relationship with the health care access, health budget per capita was positive associated with health care access, and growth in the number of consultations also had a positive relationship with the health care access. The results suggest a negative correlation between health care access and health management performance. While the bed occupancy rate was negatively associated with health management performance, and health budget per capita was positively associated with health management performance. From research results, this study has proposed policy implications to contribute to increase the health care access and promote the health management performance.

Keywords: Average days per inpatient, healthcare, health care access, healthcare expenditures, health budget per capita, health management performance.

1. INTRODUCTION

The relationship between health care access and the health management performance is an important consideration in the healthcare. The health care access represented as the number of consultations, and it refers to the convenience with which an individual can get needed medical services. The average days per inpatient refer as an indicator of the health management performance, and it is thus becoming increasingly important to catch up with the rising healthcare demands.

Along with a robust economic growth, Vietnam has now been facing a rise in public healthcare demand as it strives to ensure the health care access in order to achieve the goals towards universal health coverage. The network of medical facilities has been developed widely, which has helped improve all the indicators of health and average life expectancy. However, high demand for healthcare means that hospitals are still overcrowded and under-resourced. The network of medical at the grassroots level still has a range of limitations. The demand for healthcare is significantly greater than the availability of doctors and nurses, the medical equipment and medicines. Therefore, the network of medical at the grassroots level has built and developed in many years. This was a project that focused on the medical equipment and medicines, material facilities, professional skills, human resources. At the same time, the government promulgates the investment incentive policies in health care services to serve the patients, prevent the overcrowding in the national level hospitals, increase health care access, and improve health management performance. The knowledge gap is identified when this study systematically examines previous studies in Vietnam, and showed that there are no studies on the relationship between health care access and health management performance. Therefore, the knowledge gap that this study aims to fill is the study of factors influencing the health care access and health management performance, and the relationship between them.

This study collected the health data from the Ministry of health and General statistics office of Vietnam for the years 1990 - 2019, and conducted to analyze the impact factors in two models through applied a quantitative approach. The main purpose of this research is to develop an in-depth understanding of the impact factors on the health care access and the health management performance, and found there was significant interaction between them on positive trends. The study results have implications for health care services, and contribute to the theoretical and experimental on the health care access and the health management performance. The conclusions that this study draw from the results and explain the findings may be important for the policy, practice, theory, and subsequent research. In which, the policy implications include the rational distribution further for investing and spending in human resource, science, technology in health care services; these contribute to increase the health care access and improve the health management performance. Therefore, it again shows that this research is more urgent to explore the factors influencing the health care access and the health management performance. In particular, the findings and the policy implications created an opportunity for the policy-makers, stakeholders, and hospitals contribute to achieve the goals towards universal health coverage.

2. LITERATURE REVIEW

2.1. Health Care Access

There are many definitions of the health care access; in which, the health care access meant the timely use of health services to achieve the best health outcomes. The definition identify those areas of medical care in which the health care services showed to influence health status, and it relied on the use of health care services and health outcomes (Millman, 1993). The health care access should encompass prevention, diagnosis, disease management, and palliative care in the whole continuum of care. The health care access in the widest sense, including access to other services in connection with the personal health as public healthcare services, to social care services, community care, and support (EPF, 2016). The health care access was measured by the number of patients served at a general practitioner practice and the number of patients who have had a check-up in a given year. In the other words, the health care access represented as the number of consultations for the patients (EXPH, 2018). The health care access included the four components that were coverage, services, timeliness, and workforce. In which, coverage was the component that facilitated entry into the health care system. Uninsured people are less likely to receive medical care and more likely to have poor health status; the services was the component that has a usual source of care is associated with adults receiving recommended screening and prevention services; the timeliness was the component that created ability to provide health care when the need is recognized; the workforce was the component that included capable, qualified, culturally competent providers (HealthyPeople, 2020). Therefore, the health care access is a measure that reflects the whole continuum of health care, it represented as the number of consultations for the patients and influenced by the following factors:

Firstly, health management performance: The health management performance was measured by the average days per inpatient. Because, The average days per inpatient referred to the average number of days that patients stayed in hospital, and it was often used as an indicator of efficiency. Decreased the average days per inpatient results in decreased risks of opportunistic infections, improvement in the quality of treatment, and increased the health management performance. The number of treated patients with longer hospital stays indicated that the hospitals were not operating effectively. This led to a high bed occupancy rate and adversely affected people's health care access (Baillie et al., 1997). One of the reasons for health care access problems was the long average duration of treatment. This showed the average days per inpatient had a negative impact on the health care access (De Pietro et al., 2015). Prolonged stay in the hospitals disrupted the patient flow and access to care due to bed shortages (Toh, Lim, Yap, & Tang, 2017). This showed that the increase in the health management performance contributed to increase the health care access. Since the clients wre giving increasing emphasis to the quality of living, the hospitals should concentrated on quality improvement, continued their commitment to improve the health management performance, improve treatment outcomes, effort towards high value interventions. Thereby, the health management performance contributed to improve the health care access (Ha & Ha, 2020).

Hypothesis 1.1 (H1.1): Health management performance has positive effect on health care access.

Secondly, health workforce: The delivery of health care is highly dependent upon the availability of trained health workforce. Health workforce used the new skills and knowledge to improve health care access (WMA, 2006). Lack of personnel was highlighted in the hospitals, and this had negative effects in both quantitative and qualitative terms for the health care access (Economou, 2015). The health workforce was the cornerstone of the hospitals, playing a central role in providing health care to the population, and was crucial for ensuring access to health care for the whole population (OECD, 2016). Strategies to increase the universal health coverage that was to increase the coverage of health workforce at the hospitals. Therefore, The health workforce was a key component of any the hospitals and was a key factor for improving the health care access (Jin, Zhu, Yuan, & Meng, 2017). The hospitals and practitioners interested in the health workforce, created the healthy working and the treatment environment, generated a wealth of applied knowledge, concentrated to advance professional skills and professional qualifications of the health workforce that contributed to improve the health care access (Ha & Ha, 2020). The hospitals created the favorable conditions to increase the health care access, created many favorable conditions for people to learn and understand the health promotion to cope with the chronic illness and injuries was essential through the reorientation of health services, increased an interest in the health workforce, as well as changed in the professional instruction and training for the health workforce (Ha & Ha, 2021).

Hypothesis 1.2 (H1.2): health workforce has positive effect on health care access.

Thirdly, growth in the number of consultations: The healthcare network, rural health centres and the surgeries, and the few urban health centres were expanded that contributed to increase the growth in the number of consultations, and this was a significant determinant of the health care access (Economou, 2015). The hospitals should concentrate on quality improvement, continue their commitment to improve the quality of health care services. This contributed to increase the growth in the number of consultations, and had a positive impact on the health care access (Ha & Ha, 2020). The health care services were provided quickly and promptly, respond to patients' health status immediately that contributed to increase the growth in the number of consultations. Thereby, the hospitals contributed to improve the health care access, and facilitate the effective disease prevention (Ha & Ha, 2021).

Hypothesis 1.3 (H1.3): growth in the number of consultations *has positive effect on health care access.*

Fourthly, health budget per capita: The way a health care system was organized, in particular the design of health budget, were likely to have impact on health expenditure. A larger share of health budget per capita would allow better access to health care services which in turn may increase utilization and total health cost (Xu, Saksenaa, & Holly, 2011). Economic growth contributed to increase in both private and public spending on health, and the health budget per capita; as a result, people's access to needed health services continued to progress in all regions of the world (Xu et al., 2019). In response to the rapid change in the needs of disease prevention and health care access, the hospitals performed invariably involved in operation re-engineering by actively equipment and facilities enhancement. The hospitals provided modern equipment and facilities systems to facilitate better treatment that allow people to access quickly, effectively, and safely in the disease prevention. Accordingly, the hospitals increased to invest modern equipment and facilities systems, and this led to increase the health budget per capita (Ha & Ha, 2021).

Hypothesis 1.4 (H1.4): Health budget per capita has positive effect on health care access.

Fifthly, healthcare expenditures per total gross domestic product (GDP): The imposition of public health spending restrictions had negative effects, especially for middle-and low-income households that lack the disposable income to buy private health services (Economou, 2015). This showed the healthcare expenditures per total GDP had a positive impact on the health care access.
Pursue efficient health financing policies to respond to unmet needs and to eliminate financial barriers to access to essential health services, medicines, vaccines, diagnostics and health technologies for all throughout the life course, through better allocation and use of resources, with adequate financing for the health care services (Xu et al., 2019). The healthcare expenditures per total GDP of countries varied in terms of economic development. The healthcare expenditure was considered an investment in human capital, and an increase in healthcare expenditure could lead to regular health interventions; this, in turn, would increase the health care access (Raghupathi & Raghupathi, 2020).

Hypothesis 1.5 (H1.5): Healthcare expenditures per total GDP has positive effect on health care access.

2.2. Health Management Performance

The health management performance literature lacks consensus on concepts and definitions. In which, the measures and indicators in the health management performance was evident in the literature and in practice such as acute patients in over 30 days, length of stay, bed usage, etc (Van Peursem, Prat, & Lawrence, 1995). The length of stay was an important performance indicator for hospital management and a key measure of efficiency of the hospitals, and it was a high-level performance indicator performance assessment that was central to the drive for higher quality standards within the hospitals (Kulinskaya, Kornbrot, & Gao, 2005). The health management performance was measured by the average days per inpatient. Targets in the health management performance were to improve access to health services, in particular waiting times, and the patient and user experience (Smith, Mossialos, Papanicolas, & Leatherman, 2009). The health management performance referred to how far health care systems achieve each of the goals (Durán, Kutzin, Martin-Moreno, & Travis, 2011). The length of stay was an important indicator of the efficiency of health care management. Reduction in the number of inpatient days results in improvement in the quality of treatment, and increased the health management performance (Baek et al., 2018). The hospital management performance indicators were used as variables in the study such as bed turnover rate and average length of stay (Yiğit, 2019). This study use the average days per inpatient to measure the health management performance, decreased the average days per inpatient results in decreased risks of opportunistic infections, improvement in the quality of treatment, and increased the health management performance, and the average days per inpatient influenced by the following factors.

Firstly, bed occupancy rate: High bed occupancy rates suggested that could adversely affect safe, effective hospital function, when it was above 85%, and had a negative impact on the health management performance (Keegan, 2010). High bed occupancy rates had a negative impact on the health management performance, it caused bed shortages, and increased average days per inpatien (Madsen, Ladelund, & Linneberg, 2014). The bed occupancy rate utilization was influenced by various factors, and it was one of the important indicators that influenced the health management performance (Yiğit, 2019). The bed occupancy rate was an important indicator tracked across the hospitals. Forecasting bed occupancy rate helped the hospitals to efficiently manage the treatment operation (Tan, Ng, Nguyen, & Lam, 2019).

Hypothesis 2.1 (H2.1): Bed occupancy rate has a negative effect on health management performance.

Secondly, growth in the number of consultations: As the demand for the healthcare services has increased, many people have joined the health care program, and growth in the number of consultations resulted in significant increased length of stay of the patients (Qureshi, Ghawanni, Bakhider, & AlDarrab, 2010). This reflected growth in the number of consultations had a negative impact on the health management performance. Increasing in the number of consultations was followed by longer length of stay (Casalino et al., 2019). This showed growth in the number of consultations had a negative impact on the health management performance. The patients that had the highest number of consultations were infants and the elderly, and growth in the number of consultations associated with many factors, including the average days per inpatient (Zhao et al., 2020). Growth in the number of consultations as well as early palliative care consultation was significantly associated with shorter mean length of stay (Pottash, McCamey, Groninger, Aulisi, & Chang, 2020). This indicated that growth in the number of consultations had a positive impact on the health management performance.

Hypothesis 2.2 (H2.2): Growth rate of insured people has a positive or negative effect on health management performance.

Thirdly, health budget per capita: There was a relationship between budgeting practice and the performance of the health sector, and the health management performance to be positively associated with the use of budgets (King, Clarkson, & Wallace, 2010). The average length of stay had decreased in hospitals and this decline was offset by an increase in health budget per capita. This showed that an increase the health budget per capita could lead to increase the health management performance (Zhao et al., 2020). The hospitals increased to invest modern equipment and facilities systems, and this led to increase the health budget per capita, and contributed to increase the health management performance (Ha & Ha, 2021).

Hypothesis 2.3 (H2.3): Health budget per capita has a positive effect on on health management performance.

Fourthly, healthcare expenditures per total GDP: There was the relationship between health spending and GDP, the health expenditures in various countries were differentially impacted by the factors, and the goal of health expenditures was to provide access to medically appropriate and medically effective services. This showed that the health management performance was impacted by the healthcare expenditures per total GDP (Schieber, 1990). There was some evidence of relationship between spending and the health management performance, and this could indicate healthcare expenditures per total GDP had a negative impact on the average days per inpatient (Puozaa, 2016). Healthcare expenditures was related to average hospital stay, reducing healthcare expenditures could create benefits and increase the health management performance. This could show that reducing healthcare expenditures per total GDP contribute to increase the health management performance (Soong, Gillam, Bornstein, & Navarro, 2017).

Hypothesis 2.4 (H2.4): Healthcare expenditures per total GDP has a positive or negative effect on health management performance.

Fifthly, health care access (number of consultations): The average days per inpatient was one approach to improving clinical performance, and the admissions were associated with increased the average days per inpatient. In other words, the number of consultations were associated with the health management performance, and it had a negative impact on the health management performance (Earnest, Chen, &

Seow, 2006). In long stay patients, having fewer inpatient consultations. This showed the number of consultations had a negative impact on the average days per inpatient (Schmocker et al., 2016). In other words, the number of consultations had a positive impact on the health management performance. The study found significant associations between consultation and treatment efficiency, and a short consultation length was likely to adversely affect patient healthcare and treatment efficiency (Irving et al., 2017). The health management performance, in particular the average days per inpatient, was influenced by a number of factors, such as time for conducting consultation services and number of consultations (Ravaghi, Alidoost, Mannion, & Bélorgeot, 2020).

Hypothesis 2.5 (H2.5): Health care access has a positive or negative *effect on health management performance.*

This study formulates the following hypotheses that focus on the two models that factors affecting health care access and factors affecting health management performance.

as can be seen in Figure 1.

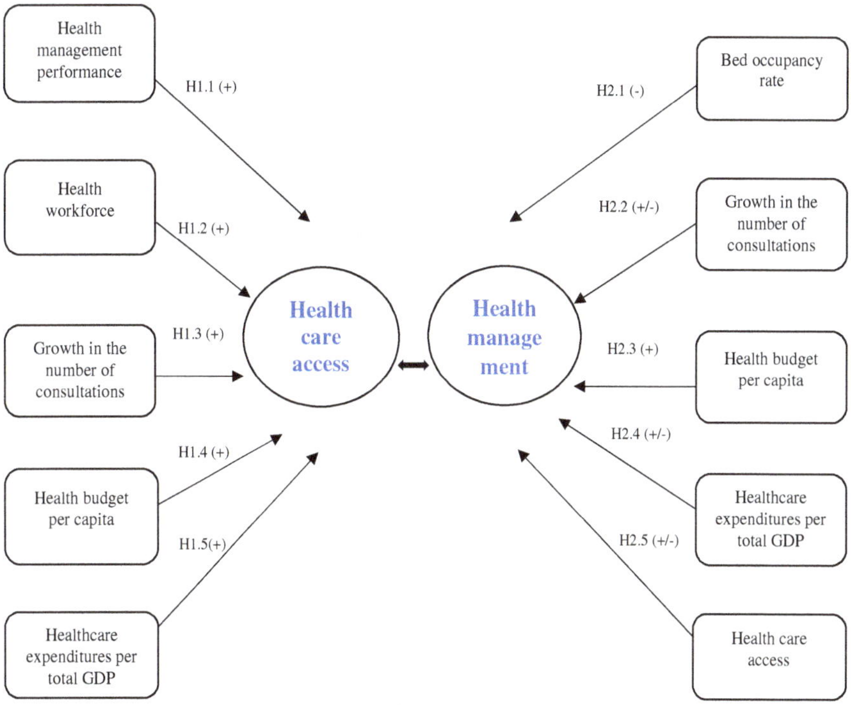

Figure 1. The relationships of the hypotheses

3. METHODS

This study collected health data from Vietnam health statistics yearbook of the Ministry of health and the statistical yearbook of General statistics office of Vietnam in the period of 1990 - 2019. The analysis models of factors affecting health care access and factors affecting health management performance were established as follows:

$$Y_1 = \alpha_{10} + \alpha_{11}Y_2 + \sum_{k=1}^{n} \beta_{1k}X_{1k} + \mu_1 \quad (1)$$

$$Y_2 = \alpha_{20} + \alpha_{21}Y_1 + \sum_{\gamma=1}^{m} \beta_{2\gamma}X_{2\gamma} + \mu_2 \quad (2)$$

Where,

Y_1 is a variable that measures the health care access, determined by the number of consultations. Y_2 is a variable that measures the health management performance, determined by the average days of stay in the hospital per admitted patient. X_{1k}, and $X_{2\gamma}$ are the independent variables that can affect the health care access and the health management performance in Equation 1 and Equation 2, respectively.The coefficient α and coefficient β are the correlation coefficients, and μ is the regression residual. For simplicity, indicator i shows the number of observations and indicator t shows the number observed year. This study used Stata 15.0 software with the variables described briefly and the definitions of the variables and their expected signs as shown in Table 1.

Table 1. *Summary of the research model variables*

Variables and symbols	Definition	Expected sign and hypotheses
Factors affecting health care access		
Dependent variable		
Health care access (HCA)	The number of consultations: The number of contacts with physicians	
Independent variables		
Health management performance (HMP)	Average days per inpatient: Total Patient days during the	H1.1: + (high AID, high HCA)

	given period / Number of discharges during that period	
Health workforce (HW)	Doctors and assistant doctors per 10000 inhabitants	H1.2: + (high HW, high HCA)
Growth in the number of consultations (GNC)	Growth in the number of consultations	H1.3: + (high GNC, high HCA)
Health budget per capita (HBC)	Health budget / Population	H1.4: + (high HBC, high HCA)
Healthcare expenditures per total GDP (HEG)	Healthcare expenditures / Total GDP	H1.5: + (high HEG, high HCA)
Factors affecting health management performance		
Dependent variable		
Health management performance (HMP)	Average days per inpatient: Total Patient days during the given period / Number of discharges during that period	
Independent variable		
Bed occupancy rate (BOR)	(Daily average of beds occupied / Bed complement) x 100	H2.1: - (high BOR, low HMP)
Growth in the number of consultations (GNC)	Growth in the number of consultations	H2.2: +/- (high GNC, high or low HMP)
Health budget per capita (HBC)	Health budget / Population	H2.3: + (high HBC, high HMP)
Healthcare expenditures per total GDP (HEG)	Healthcare expenditures / Total GDP	H2.4: +/- (high HEG, high or low HMP)
Health care access (HCA)	The number of consultations: The number of contacts with physicians	H2.5: +/- (high HCA, high or low HMP)

This study applied multivariate regression, it is used to predict the value of the variables HCA (y_1) and HMP (y_2). This variables called the dependent variables, while the variables that are termed as independent variables including HMP, HW, GNC, HBC and HEG that used to calculate the dependent variable HCA, and the variables BOR, GIP, HBC, HEG and HCA that used to calculate the dependent variable HMP. Correlation analysis was carried out on each variable, and used to evaluate the strength of relationship between the quantitative variables in the models. The study conducted testing for multicollinearity with variance inflation factors (VIF) to identify correlation between independent variables and the strength of that correlation. At the same time, checking residual variance change, and the tests for auto-correlation were conducted in these research models.

4. RESULTS

4.1. Descriptive Statistics

The descriptive statistics results found that the BOR, HBC, HCA, HEG, HMP and HW variables had smaller standard deviations than the average, this showes that the values tend to be close to the mean of the variables. The descriptive statistics results found that the BOR, HBC, HCA, HEG, HMP and HW variables had smaller standard deviations than the average, this showes that the values tend to be close to the mean of the variables. The healthcare system in Vietnam has gradually decreased the bed occupancy rate over the years, and it had the lowest was 128.97 and the highest achieveed 102.17. The health budget per capita has gradually increased over the years, and the health expenditures included healthcare goods and services consumed and increased during each year. While the health care access had many fluctuations over the years. The health management performance has gradually increased over the years, and this indicator had the lowest point of 1.39 and the highest was 7.35. The annual increase in the number of trained health workforce have added to the human resources of hospitals and contributed to increase the health workforce per 10,000 inhabitants; and these indicators obtained 11.99 of the lowest and the highest attained 14.3. On the other hand, the growth in the number of consultations had many fluctuations over the years due to changes in health insurance programs and health systems in each period as can be seen in Table 2.

Table 2. *Descriptive statistics*

Variable	Mean	Std. Dev.	Min	Max
BOR	113.6643	7.88817	102.17	128.97
GNC	.0049788	.0463485	-.0625493	.084888
HBC	1379.357	763.3927	586.5	2951
HCA	208204.4	8301.532	196456.6	229775.7
HEG	3.444286	.4295027	2.63	4.02
HMP	6.107143	2.012237	1.39	7.35
HW	13.32929	.7648174	11.99	14.3

Source: Authors' calculation from Stata 15.0.

4.2. Correlation Analysis

The analysis results of correlation between variables was smaller than .70 (-.70). These results showed that the degree of correlation between the variables from negligible correlation to the moderate correlation. Because, the size of a correlation coefficient showed that moderate positive (negative) correlation with size of correlation from .50 to .70 (−.50 to −.70); the size of correlation from .30 to .50 (−.30 to −.50) was the low positive (negative) correlation; the size of correlation from .00 to .30 (.00 to −.30) was the negligible correlation (Hinkle, Wiersma, & Jurs, 2003). Therefore, the presence of any multicollinearity was neglected in the models, as can be seen in Table 3.

Table 3. *Correlation matrix*

Correlation matrix for factors affecting health care access						
	HCA	HMP	HW	GNC	HBC	HEG
HCA	1.0000					
HMB	-0.0438	1.0000				
HW	0.5611	-0.2203	1.0000			
GNC	0.5934	0.0885	0.0822	1.0000		
HBC	0.5230	-0.5329	0.5142	-0.0120	1.0000	
HEG	0.5008	-0.5305	0.6409	0.0393	0.5447	1.0000
Correlation matrix for factors affecting health management performance						
	HMP	BOR	GNC	HBC	HEG	HCA
HMP	1.0000					
BOR	0.6453	1.0000				
GNC	0.0885	0.0109	1.0000			
HBC	-0.5329	-0.1871	-0.0120	1.0000		
HEG	-0.5305	-0.0217	0.0393	0.5447	1.0000	
HCA	-0.0438	0.1609	0.5934	0.5230	0.5008	1.0000

Source: Authors' calculation from Stata 15.0.

4.3. Regression Results

In the model of factors affecting health care access showed the variables HMP, GNC and HBC had positive impacts on the variable HCA at the significance level of 10%, 5% and 10%, respectively. The variable HEG had a positive impact on the variable HCA, and the variable HW had a negative impact on the variable HCA, but these variables were not statistically significant in this mode as can be seen in Table 4. The study examined multicollinearity for factors affecting BOR had a result of Mean VIF = 3.66, VIF of variables from 1.02 to 3.73, this indicated no serious multicollinearity in this model. Checking residual variance change with P-value = 0.3758 was greater than 0.05, therefore, there was not the variance change phenomenon in this model. Checking serial correlation with P-value = 0.0905 was greater than 0.05, therefore, there was not the serial correlation in this model.

Table 4. *Regression results for factors affecting health care access*

Independent variables	Dependent variable (HCA)
HMP	3335.3*
	(3.08)
HW	-2931.7
	(-1.03)
GNC	98294.9**
	(3.99)
HBC	12.45*
	(3.10)
HEG	4421.1
	(1.08)
_cons	194025.9***
	(6.65)

Notes: ***, **, * denote significance at the level of 1%, 5% and 10%
Source: Compiled from data processing results of Stata software

In the model of factors affecting health management performance found the variables BOR and HCA had positive relationships with the variable HMP at the significance level of 10% and 10%, respectively. The variable HBC had negative relationship with the variable HMP at the significance level of 5%. The variables GNC, and HEG had negative relationships with the variable HMP, but these variables were not statistically significant in this mode as can be seen in Table 5. The study examined multicollinearity for factors affecting ADI had a result of Mean VIF = 2.50, VIF of variables from 1.28 to 3.40, this indicated no serious multicollinearity in this model. Checking residual variance change with P-value = 0.3738 was greater than 0.05, therefore, there was not the variance change phenomenon in this model. Checking serial correlation with P-value = 0.3653 was greater than 0.05, therefore, there was not the serial correlation in this model.

Table 5. *Regression results for factors affecting health management performance*

Independent variables	Dependent variable (HMP)
BOR	0.102*
	(3.31)
GNC	-10.86
	(-1.58)
HBC	-0.00215**
	(-4.25)
HEG	-8.63
	(-1.11)

HCA	0.000136*
	(2.82)
_cons	-27.76*
	(-3.23)

Notes: ***, **, * denote significance at the level of 1%, 5% and 10%
Source: Compiled from data processing results of Stata software

5. DISCUSSIONS

The results in Table 4 showed that the average days per inpatient had a positive impact on the health care access with coefficient 3335.3, and with the significance level of 10%. This result showed that for one unit increased in the health management performance, the health care access was anticipated to reduce by 3335.3 units, when the remaining variables in the model were kept constant. This result disagreed with the analysis results of Baillie et al. (1997), De Pietro et al. (2015), Toh, Lim, Yap and Tang (2017), and Ha and Ha (2020). The health management performance has gradually increased over the years, and this indicator had the lowest point of 1.39 and the highest was 7.35. The health management performance has gradually increased over the years, and this indicator had the lowest point of 1.39 and the highest was 7.35. Nevertheless, the numbers of patients being treated that had the longer lengths of stay in hospital caused the high average number of days that patients spent in the hospitals, and overcrowding in hospitals is one of the problems that the healthcare sector must solve in order to further decrease the average number of days that patients spent in the hospitals. Thereby, the reduction in the number of inpatient days results in the improvement in the quality of the treatment, and increases the bed turnover rate, and the hospitals contribute to promote the health care access.

The outcome of the regression analysis indicated the growth in the number of consultations had a coefficient 98294.9 with the significance level of 5%. This showed that increasing in the number of consultations improved the health care access by 98294.9 units per year. As expected, this result was broadly in harmony with the expected sign and hypotheses, and agreed with the study of Economou (2015), OECD (2016), Jin, Zhu, Yuan and Meng (2017), Ha and Ha (2020), and Ha and Ha (2021). Although the growth in the number of consultations has fluctuated over the years, it was still increasing in 2019 compared to previous years due to the health care delivery system had undergone great change, and the availability of newer and improved health-care services. The number of consultations reflects the need for health care, people obtain care, and can be accessed the health care services. So, the growth in the number of consultations contributes to promote the health care access.

The outcome of the regression analysis indicated there was a statistically significant effect of the the health budget per capita on the health care access. As expected, the study noted a coefficient that was significant at the 10% level. This result showed that for one unit increase in the health budget per capita, the health care access was anticipated to increase by 12.45 units, when the remaining variables in the model were kept constant. As expected, this result was broadly in harmony with the expected sign and hypotheses, and agreed with the study of Xu, Saksenaa and Holly (2011), Xu et al.(2019), Ha and Ha (2021). As of figures from 2019, there were over 13,550 health facilities, in branch, provincial, and national levels. This showed the healthcare system in Vietnam has a sizeable number of hospitals across the country. However, 75% of them were built more than 22 years ago, and shortage of medicines and medical equipments for critical care, and intensive care units werw also some problems that the healthcare sector have been dealing with. Ensure effective access to healthcare and improve the quality and availability of healthcare services by increasing the health budget per capita to invests and developing the facilities, medicines and medical equipments. This contributes to reduce the overcrowding in hospitals, and promote the health care access.

The results in Table 5 indicated that bed occupancy rate had a positive relationship with the average days per inpatient with coefficient 0.102, and with the significance level of 10%. This result showed that for one unit increased in the bed occupancy rate, the health management performance was anticipated to decrease by 0.102 units, when the remaining variables in the model were kept constant. As expected, this result was broadly in harmony with the expected sign and hypotheses, and agreed with the findings of Keegan (2010), Madsen, Ladelund and Linneberg (2014), Yiğit (2019), and Tan, Ng, Nguyen and Lam (2019). The overcrowding in hospitals led to an increase in the bed occupancy rate, and many patients have to wait in a hallway for days before a bed becomes available. The bed occupancy rate is always 100 percent higher in the healthcare system, especially at the provincial and city levels in Vietnam, while the bed occupancy rate of above 85 percent was generally reflected to have bed shortages (Madsen et al., 2014). The high bed occupancy rate resulted from an increase patient, and the average days per inpatient were relatively longer. This might affect the healthcare quality, lead to a risk for the patients as well as restrict the health management performance.

The model result exhibited a significant effect of the health budget per capita on the average days per inpatient, and the coefficient was negative and statistically significant at the 5 level. This result showed that for one unit increase in the health budget per capita, the health management performance was anticipated to increase by 0.00215 units, when the remaining variables in the model were kept constant. As expected, this result was broadly in harmony with the expected sign and hypotheses, and agreed with the study of King, Clarkson and Wallace (2010), Zhao et al. (2020), Ha and Ha (2021). The health management performance involved the health budget per capita, and to prevent overcrowding in hospitals, the government continued to finance the investment of new hospitals. Because, overcrowding in hospitals results in a strain on the infrastructure of healthcare facilities. In the other hand, many hospitals need to maintain and upgrade the facilities as most of them were invest more than two decades ago and need to be upgraded. The health budget per capita per capita has increased in over the years, and it was close to USD130 per capita in 2019. Therefore, the increased health budget per capita per capita increased the health management performance.

The regression result indicated a very significant effect of the health care access on the average days per inpatient, and the coefficient was positive and statistically significant at the 10% level. This result showed that for one unit increase in the health care access, the health management performance was anticipated to decrease by 0.000136 units, when the remaining variables in the model were kept constant. This result agreed with the study of Chen and Seow (2006), and was not broadly in harmony with the study of Schmocker et al. (2016), Irving et al. (2017), and Ravaghi, Alidoost, Mannion and Bélorgeot (2020). To increased in the health care access, many hospitals increase the number of consultations. This resulted in the overcrowding in hospitals, many patients being treated that had the longer lengths of stay in hospital, and a high bed occupancy rate that is always 100 percent higher in the healthcare system, especially at the provincial and city levels in Vietnam. From there, increased in the health care access lead to restrict the health management performance.

6. CONCLUSIONS AND RECOMMENDATIONS

The health care access is a measure that reflects the whole continuum of health care, it represented as the number of consultations for the patients, and increasing in the health care access is one of the goals towards universal health coverage. The health management performance was measured by the average days per inpatient, and increasing in the health management performance contributed to improve the quality of treatment and restrict the overcrowding in hospitals. This study examined the relationship between the health care access and health management performance of the healthcare system in Vietnam. Multiple regression analysis was applied in the study to find out the potential factors that affect the health care access and health management performance. The two prominent models have been identified and these research results were accurate according to the characteristics, and the development history of the Vietnamese health system in the period 1990 - 2019.

The study results found that the two factors that had positive relationships with the health care access were the growth in the number of consultations, and the health budget per capita. A factors that had a negative relationship with the health care access was the health management performance. This study also found that the two factors that had negative relationships with the health management performance were the bed occupancy rate, and the health care access. A factors that had a positive relationship with the health management performance was the health budget per capita. This study can conclude that two dependence variables of the two models were statistically significant, and there was relationship between the health care access and health management performance in a negative trend.

Nowadays, Vietnam health care system widely coverage from central to grassroots levels, and the healthcare are having a significant investment prospects in many regions of the country. This study helps the researchers, investors, and managers develop their expertise in the key determinants of the health care access and the health management performance, and the relationships of them. From the research results, the article recommends the following to increase the health care access and the health management performance.

Firstly, The hospitals should have the responsible for monitoring access to personal health services . These efforts should include the responsibility to conduct their own analyses of access indicators. At the same time, they need to improve their treatment capacity, assistance and consultation to reduce the average number of days that patients spent in the hospitals. Thereby, the hospitals create a positive interaction between the health management performance and the health care access.

Secondly, Vietnam healthcare system widely coverage from central to grassroots levels, and targets to make healthcare system universal for all people. The healthcare system has been remarkably improved along with investment facilities. Nevertheless, the health budget per capita is still low and total budget for health has not yet met the health care needs. Therefore, Vietnam healthcare system should increase the health budget per capita to invest the the infrastructure of healthcare facilities and the new hospitals to prevent overcrowding in hospitals, and better respond to health care needs. This contributes to improve the health care access, and achieve the goal of making the healthcare system universal for all people.

Thirdly, investment for the healthcare system does not meet the growing demand of health care services, beside investment the the infrastructure of healthcare facilities and the new hospitals, the healthcare system should stress the significance of renovation of the healthcare system in Vietnam, perform the efficient exploitation of all resources, use all resources to the fullest potential. Thereby, it helps to reduce the bed occupancy rate and overcrowding in hospitals, restrict to use many resourcesthe country achieve the target of universal health care coverage.

Fourthly, with the high bed occupancy rate and the healthcare system continues to far exceed the 80 percent bed occupancy rate, and a high average days per inpatient. So, the hospitals should realize that increasing bed occupancy rate will not solve the problem of hospital overcrowding. They need focuses on determining the optimal number of beds to allocate to each their unit, and should consider alternative approaches to planning hospital capacity to fix the limitations of bed occupancy rate.

Fifthly, the health care sccess is essential for the whole population, requires systematic consideration to ensure appropriate conditions are met. Based on the results identified in the study, the hospitals may be necessary to improve the approaches to promote the effective use of hospital resources and reduce the unnecessary hospital stays is a strategy to increase the bed turnover rate, and contribute to improve the health care access and the health management performance.

Sixthly, the disease patterns have been changed following the trend that many diseases have increased in recent years; in particular, new epidemic diseases such as SARS, influenza - H5N1, coronavirus - covid 19 and their variants have made situation to be worsen. This showed that the healthcare system more efforts will be needed to increase the health care access, and get universal health coverage. The healthcare system should concentrate investing in resource, science, technology in healthcare, and allocate resources more reasonably. The health care sector should increase to invest new technologies, the modern diagnostic and therapeutic equipment and new interventional medical procedures will contribute to faster and more efficient treatment, and help the hospitals possible for complex interventions to be undertaken in treatment. From there, the hospitals will reduce the average days per inpatient, increase the bed turnover rate, and contribute to improve the health care access and the health management performance.

References

Baek, H., Cho, M., Kim, S., Hwang, H., Song, M., & Yoo, S. (2018). Analysis of length of hospital stay using electronic health records: A statistical and data mining approach. *PloS one, 13*(4), e0195901.

Baillie, H., Wright, W., McLeod, A., Craig, N., Leyland, A., Drummond, N., & Boddy, A. (1997). *Bed occupancy and bed management.* University of Glasgow: Public Health Research Unit.

Casalino, E., Perozziello, A., Choquet, C., Curac, S., Leroy, C., & Hellmann, R. (2019). Evaluation of hospital length of stay and revenues as a function of admission mode, clinical pathways including observation unit stay and hospitalization characteristics. *Health services management research, 32*(1), 16-25.

De Pietro, C., Camenzind, P., Sturny, I., Crivelli, L., Edwards-Garavoglia, S., Spranger, A., . . . Quentin, W. (2015). Switzerland: Health system review. *Health Systems in Transition, 17*(4), 1-288.

Durán, A., Kutzin, J., Martin-Moreno, J. M., & Travis, P. (2011). Understanding health systems: scope, functions and objectives. *Health systems: Health, wealth, society and wellbeing. Maidenhead, Open University Press and McGraw-Hill*, 19-36.

Earnest, A., Chen, M. I., & Seow, E. (2006). Exploring if day and time of admission is associated with average length of stay among inpatients from a tertiary hospital in Singapore: an analytic study based on routine admission data. *BMC Health Services Research, 6*(1), 1-8.

Economou, C. (2015). Barriers and facilitating factors in access to health services in Greece. *Copenhagen: WHO Regional Office for Europe.*

EPF. (2016). *Defining and Measuring Access to Healthcare: the Patients' Perspective*. Belgium: European Union.

EXPH. (2018). *Opinion on tools and methodologies for assessing the performance of primary care*. Luxembourg: European Union.

Ha, V. D., & Ha, P. T. K. (2020). The impact of sustainability in health care service on client loyalty. *Journal of Critical Reviews, 7*(18), 4266-4278.

Ha, P. T. K., & Ha, V. D. (2021). The Effect of Health Promotion on Disease Prevention. *European Journal of Molecular & Clinical Medicine, 8*(2), 767-780.

HealthyPeople. (2020). Access to Health Services. Retrieved from https://www.healthypeople.gov/2020/topics-objectives/topic/Access-to-Health-Services

Hinkle, D. E., Wiersma, W., & Jurs, S. G. (2003). *Applied statistics for the behavioral sciences* (Vol. 663): Houghton Mifflin College Division.

Irving, G., Neves, A. L., Dambha-Miller, H., Oishi, A., Tagashira, H., Verho, A., & Holden, J. (2017). International variations in primary care physician consultation time: a systematic review of 67 countries. *BMJ open, 7*(10), e017902.

Jin, Y., Zhu, W., Yuan, B., & Meng, Q. (2017). Impact of health workforce availability on health care seeking behavior of patients with diabetes mellitus in China. *International journal for equity in health, 16*(1), 1-10.

Keegan, A. D. (2010). Hospital bed occupancy: more than queuing for a bed. *Medical Journal of Australia, 193*(5), 291-293.

King, R., Clarkson, P. M., & Wallace, S. (2010). Budgeting practices and performance in small healthcare businesses. *Management Accounting Research, 21*(1), 40-55.

Kulinskaya, E., Kornbrot, D., & Gao, H. (2005). Length of stay as a performance indicator: robust statistical methodology. *IMA Journal of Management Mathematics, 16*(4), 369-381.

Madsen, F., Ladelund, S., & Linneberg, A. (2014). High levels of bed occupancy associated with increased inpatient and thirty-day hospital mortality in Denmark. *Health Affairs, 33*(7), 1236-1244.

Millman, M. (1993). *Access to Health Care in America.* Washington DC: National Academies Press.

OECD. (2016). *Health Workforce Policies in OECD Countries: Right Jobs, Right Skills, Right Places.* Paris: OECD Health Policy Studies, OECD Publishing.

Pottash, M., McCamey, D., Groninger, H., Aulisi, E. F., & Chang, J. J. (2020). Palliative Care Consultation and Effect on Length of Stay in a Tertiary-Level Neurological Intensive Care Unit. *Palliative Medicine Reports, 1*(1), 161-165.

Puozaa, C. Y. (2016). The determinants of hospital length of stay in Nigeria. *International Journal of Business and Economic Sciences Applied Research (IJBESAR), 9*(3), 34-42.

Qureshi, N., Ghawanni, A., Bakhider, G., & AlDarrab, A. (2010). Consultation Impacts on patients' Length of Stay In the Emergency Department: 339. *Annals of Emergency Medicine, 53.*

Raghupathi, V., & Raghupathi, W. (2020). Healthcare Expenditure and Economic Performance: Insights From the United States Data. *Frontiers in Public Health, 8*, 156-156.

Ravaghi, H., Alidoost, S., Mannion, R., & Bélorgeot, V. D. (2020). Models and methods for determining the optimal number of beds in hospitals and regions: a systematic scoping review. *BMC Health Services Research, 20*(1), 1-13.

Schieber, G. J. (1990). Health expenditures in major industrialized countries, 1960-87. *Health care financing review, 11*(4), 159.

Schmocker, R. K., Holden, S. E., Vang, X., Lumpkin, S. T., Stafford, L. M. C., Leverson, G. E., & Winslow, E. R. (2016). The number of inpatient consultations is negatively correlated with patient satisfaction in patients with prolonged hospital stays. *The American Journal of Surgery, 212*(2), 282-288.

Smith, P. C., Mossialos, E., Papanicolas, I., & Leatherman, S. (2009). *Performance measurement for health system improvement: experiences, challenges and prospects*: Cambridge University Press.

Soong, C., Gillam, S., Bornstein, S., & Navarro, P. (2017). *Reducing Acute Care Length of Stay in Newfoundland & Labrador*. St. John's, NL: Newfoundland & Labrador Centre for Applied Health Research. Memorial University.

Tan, K. W., Ng, Q. Y., Nguyen, F. N. H. L., & Lam, S. S. W. (2019). *Data-driven decision-support for process improvement through predictions of bed occupancy rates.* Paper presented at the 2019 IEEE 15th International Conference on Automation Science and Engineering (CASE).

Toh, H. J., Lim, Z. Y., Yap, P., & Tang, T. (2017). Factors associated with prolonged length of stay in older patients. *Singapore medical journal, 58*(3), 134-138.

Van Peursem, K., Prat, M., & Lawrence, S. (1995). Health management performance: A review of measures and indicators. *Accounting, Auditing & Accountability Journal, 8*(5), 34-70.

WMA. (2006). WMA statement on access to health care. Retrieved from https://www.wma.net/policies-post/wma-statement-on-access-to-health-care/

Xu, K., Saksenaa, P., & Holly, A. (2011). *The Determinants of Health Expenditure: A Country-Level Panel Data Analysis* Geneva, Switzerland: World Health Organization.

Xu, K., Soucat, A., Kutzin, J., Siroka, A., Garcia, M. A., Dupuy, J., . . . Flores, G. (2019). *Global Spending on Health: A World in Transition*. Switzerland: World Health Organization.

Yiğit, A. (2019). Evaluation of Bed Utilization Performance of Hospital Departments in Turkey With Grey Related Analysis. *International Journal of Health Services Research and Policy, 4*(3), 173-183.

Zhao, Q., Coelho, M. S., Li, S., Saldiva, P. H., Abramson, M. J., Huxley, R. R., & Guo, Y. (2020). Trends in hospital admission rates and associated direct healthcare costs in Brazil: a nationwide retrospective study between 2000 and 2015. *Innovation, 38*(30), 1-30.

THE INTERACTION RELATIONSHIP BETWEEN THE DIVERSIFICATION OF HEALTH CARE SUPPORT ACTIVITIES AND THE HEALTH CARE SERVICES OUTREACH IN MICROFINANCE INSTITUTIONS

Pham Trong Khang Ha[1*], Van Duong Ha[2]

[1] Faculty of Medicine, University of Medicine Pham Ngoc Thach, Ho Chi Minh City, Vietnam.

[2] Saigon Institute of Economics and Technology, Ho Chi Minh City, Vietnam

E mail: [1] khangha.pt@gmail.com ; [2] dhv05@yahoo.com

***Abstract*:**

One of the main ways to strengthen the health-system capacity by the interdisciplinary approaches is to promote social health by linking microfinance with healthcare support activities. It may be greatly useful to enhance this association, and the aim of the study was to discover the interaction relationship between the diversification of health care support activities and the health care services outreach of formal microfinance institutions (MFIs) in Vietnam. This study used the panel data regression method from 2012 to 2022 of all formal MFIs in Vietnam. The results showed that number of branches and the health care services outreach had positive relationships with the diversification of health care support activities; productivity had a negative impact on the diversification of health care support activities. The diversification of health care support activities, and productivity had positive relationships with the health care services outreach; number of branches had a negative impact on the health care services outreach. At the same time, this study found bidirectional interactions and the causal relationship between the diversification of health care support activities and the health care services outreach of formal MFIs in Vietnam. This study found bidirectional interactions and the causal relationship between the diversification of health care support activities and the health care services outreach. The study results encourage and provide opportunities to diversify the health care support activities and to promote the health care services outreach of formal MFIs in Vietnam.

***Keywords*:** Health Care, Health Care Services, Health Care Support, Microfinance, Vietnam.

1. INTRODUCTION

One of the main ways to strengthen the health-system capacity by the interdisciplinary approaches is to promote social health by linking microfinance with healthcare support activities. Up to now, many countries have focused to strengthen the resources for the health system development. At the same time, they have focused on reducing the poverty gap as well as improving health. Therefore, many countries have increased to build their health-system capacity by the interdisciplinary approaches. One of the main ways that they have promoted social health is by the linking of microfinance with the healthcare support activities. MFIs expand their services to include the health care services. Because, the health care services are the extension of their mission of financial security and social protection of the clients and healthier customers better serve the MFIs' goals of growth and long-term viability. Therefore, the health care services outreach is one of the main ways that they have promoted their operational sustainability. Many MFIs have shown their ability to contribute to improving health care capacity by educating clients, facilitating access to the health care services, providing health financing options and even directly delivering clinical care. MFIs provide the health care services to many households in support of access to the health care services. Many of them live in rural and remote areas beyond the reach of the hospitals and health agencies. Many MFIs already successfully offer the health care services. Increasing numbers also provide health-related services, such as medical care, health financing, and establishing links with medical service providers to facilitate access to health care. However, MFIs offer the health care services, admittedly with challenges to employ the infrastructure for delivery of health-related services to those most in need. The poor people bear a hugely disproportionate share of disease and ill-health, and inability to access the health system emerged as key factors inducing and resulting from poverty (Leatherman and Dunford, 2010).

The studies of MFIs delivering the health care support activities showed increasing evidence of positive impact. Many studies found that adding health care instruction, health education, usually delivered during the microfinance customers group meetings, improves knowledge and creates confidence that leads to behavioural change. These behaviours are associated with positive health outcomes in diverse areas that are critically important to achieving the health care services outreach (Leatherman and Dunford, 2010). In Vietnam, the operations of formal MFIs have reached 25 provinces and cities with 176 branches and transaction offices in Vietnam. One of the significant missions of formal MFIs are the formulation of the policies that are intended to diversify the health care support activities and to promote the health care services outreach to the microfinance customers. However, to diversify the health care support activities and to promote the health care services outreach are quite the toughs and challenges for MFIs. The challenges have to face as servicing remote and sparsely populated areas, fast-paced growth needs proper infrastructural planning such as branches, transaction points, which can be dangerously inefficiency without a high degree of diversification in health care support activities, and the health care services success is limited, etc. At the same time, there are no studies on the interaction relationship between the diversification of health care support activities and the health care services outreach by MFIs in Vietnam. Addressing this gap, the study's purpose was to examine the interaction relationship between the diversification of health care support activities and the health care services outreach. The research approach is based on the diversification of health care support activities of the formal where microfinance is seen as the health care services outreach. The study used a quantitative approach using panel data from the formal MFIs from 2012 to 2022. The study results will contribute to the theoretical and experimental including aspects as this study has developed an in-depth analysis of the health care services outreach and an econometric analysis on the interaction relationship between the diversification of health care support activities and the health care services outreach; the research demonstrated that bidirectional interactions and the causal relationship between the diversification of health care support activities and the health care services outreach. Furthermore, the study offers policy implication and new insights for developing a more the health care services outreach of formal MFIs and further emphasizes optimal policies to formal MFIs management; the managers should make conscious efforts and create a balance in the achievement of the goals of health care services outreach in accomplishing the diversification of health care support activities. Therefore, this study is urgently required to balance the goals of health care services outreach. In particular, this study is helpful to decision-makers and other stakeholders of formal MFIs in Vietnam.

2. LITERATURE AND HYPOTHESES

2.1. The diversification of health care support activities

The diversification of health care support activities were defined as microfinance outreach indicator, it was measured by diversity indicators in microfinance services indicators, and it had been defined by various researchers differently. The microfinance services diversity was the number of types of microfinance services offered by MFIs (Zeller and Meyer, 2002). The microfinance services diversity was the number of types of microfinance services contracts supplied. The microfinance services diversity might mean both financial services and non-financial services. The MFIs had ample non-financial services not only because it offered the health care support activities with a variety of terms but also because it offered establishing linkages to health providers to facilitate access to health care, and even directly delivering clinical care (Schreiner, 2002). The microfinance services diversity referred to the diversity of services and products beings availed by active customers. This included variety of non-financial services (Srinivasan, 2013). The microfinance services diversity indicated the number of the types of products and services, and others offered product based on the product lines or the types of product including the number and type of offered product, difference in the number, and the type of the offered voluntary non-finance service (Primiana et al., 2018). The MFIs promoted the diversification of products and services in line with the operation trends and associated with the development of modern technology to meet the customer needs, that contribute to expand the scope of outreach of MFIs (Ha, 2020a). The number of microfinance products and services showed the number of products and service groups, the number of products and services in each microfinance product and service group. The number of microfinance products and services was manifold, the microfinance product and service diversification contributed to expand the scope of outreach to the microfinance customers. At the same time, the microfinance services diversity might mean both financial services and non-financial service. The microfinance services diversity within a non-financial services might mean educating clients, facilitating access to the health care services, providing health financing options, establishing linkages to health providers to facilitate access to health care, and even directly delivering clinical care (Hà Văn Dương, 2020a). The previous literature showed that the diversification of health care support activities can be measured in different ways. In this study, the diversification of health care support activities refers to the number of health care support activities offered to the microfinance customers. Accordingly, the diversification of health care support activities reflects the number, and type of health education, providing health programs, health promotion programs, adoption of nutrition practices, discussed family planning with spouses, health nutrition knowledge and practice among women, more attention to infant care nutrition, vaccination, etc., facilitating access to the health care services, providing health financing options, establishing linkages to health providers to facilitate access to health care, and directly delivering clinical care, and different health care support services offered by MFIs.

The diversification of health care support activities is associated with all MFIs' operations, it has been regarded as a prerequisite for continuous improvement the health care services outreach and is influenced by many factors, including:

Firstly, asset growth rate: There was a positive relationship between microfinance services and assets. Thereby, the asset growth rate had a positive relationship with the diversification of health care support activities (Zeller and Meyer, 2002). The asset growth of MFIs would contribute positively to the development of microfinance products and services, which included diversification of the health care support activities (Hà Văn Dương, 2020b).

H1.1: There is a positive relationship between the asset growth rate and the diversification of health care support activities of formal MFIs.

Secondly, number of branches: A large branch network ensured customers could access more and more convenient the microfinance services, allowing MFIs to provide the diverse microfinance services, including the health care support activities (Hubbard, 2007). Thereby, number of branches contributed to diversify the health care support activities of MFIs. Many MFIs provided microfinance services to millions of households worldwide. In particular, they provided the health care support activities a million of these households are very poor, many households are lived in remote areas beyond the reach of health agencies. Microfinance sector increased number of MFIs to offer health-related services, such as instruction, clinical care, health-financing and linkages to the health providers. This contributed to diversify the health care support activities of MFIs (Leatherman, 2012). Some MFIs had increased the number of branches, expanding the scope of the operations that had provided the variety of microfinance services and promoted diversification of the health care support activities (Ha, 2020b).

H1.2: There is a positive relationship between the number of branches and the diversification of health care support activities of formal MFIs.

Thirdly, productivity: The productivity was one of the indicators in microfinance that measured as a ratio of the number of customers to number of staff. This indicator showed how efficiently the available human resource was utilized (Rauf and Mahmood, 2009). Productivity was measured the numbers of customers per staff of MFIs (Rashid and Twaha, 2013). The staff productivity positively drove the outreach of MFIs. The results showed that the productivity appeared to be a better predictor of MFIs wider outreach. This provided an incentive for MFIs to provide a wide range of products services, including health care support activities (Abdulai and Tewari, 2017a). Hence, the productivity had a positive relationship with diversification of the health care support activities of MFIs. Microfinance initiatives have been shown to advance health outcomes. The MFIs always maintain a combination of the productivity and the health care services outreach, and an appropriate productivity growth strategy contributed to diversify the health care support activities of MFIs (Ha, 2020c).

H1.3: There is a positive relationship between the productivity and the diversification of health care support activities of formal MFIs.

Fourthly, the health care services outreach: Services outreach was the term that was used to reflect the health services that mobilized health resources to provide health services to the population in in remote and rural areas (Roodenbeke, 2011). Therefore, the health care services outreach aimed towards promoting health care services by enhancing health care delivery in communities. Through the health care service providers, communities can improve innovative approaches to challenges related to their specific health needs. Services outreach was the term that was used to reflect the health services that mobilized health resourses to provide health services to the population in remote and rural areas (Roodenbeke, 2011). Therefore, the health care services outreach aimed towards promoting health care services by enhancing health care delivery in communities. Through the health care service providers, communities can improve innovative approaches for the challenges related to their specific health needs. There are many the research on the outreach of MFIs, the outreach of MFIs was measured by the number of people a microfinance institution has extended their services over a specific period (Quayes, 2012). The outreach of MFIs was related to the actual number of microfinance customers (Rao and Fitamo, 2015). The outreach of MFIs was related to the actual number of poor people reached with services of MFIs (Abdulai and Tewari, 2017a). The outreach of MFIs concerned with the efforts to widen service for those who receive inadequate service. The indicators refer to the number of customers, the shifting percentage of served clients and either the types of products or programs (Primiana et al., 2018). The outreach of MFIs the larger the number of customers the better the outreach of MFIs. Therefore, the health care services outreach could be measured by many ways. This study used the number of customers to measure the health care services outreach (Ha, 2020c). The increase in outreach was undoubtedly to some extent the result of an increase in the services of MFIs. The outreach included the health care services outreach that refered to the goal of extending as many services as possible of MFIs (Kent and Dacin, 2013). Many MFIs have increased the outreach to meet the services needs of customers and members, The outreach of MFIs contributed to expand their operations and diversify the health care support activities of MFIs (Ha, 2020d).

H1.4: There is a positive relationship between the health care services outreach and the diversification of health care support activities of formal MFIs.

Fifthly, operational sustainability: Sustainability in the operations was the goal of many sectors and fields, each sector would rely on economic and social characteristics to plan the most suitable strategy for sustainable development. The MFIs would have operational sustainability if their revenue generated from the operations that covered the operating expenses, financing costs and loss provisions. The ability of the organizations to meet their operating cost was defined the sustainability (UNESCAP, 2007). Sustainability generally meant the ability of an ongoing program to perform activities and services in pursuit of the planned objectives. Operational sustainability of MFIs referred to the ability of MFIs to cover all of its costs through their income, and this was a tangible parameter that was measured continuously to monitor the level of income to cover all costs to ensure that MFIs would develop in long-term (Ha, 2020c). MFIs provided the poor with social services such as the health care service activities and health care instruction. They have increased social sustainability, which provided additional services to particular clientele in remote and rural areas. As a result, the operational sustainability of MFIs contribute to diversify the health care service activities to meet the growing demand of their members and customers (Sim and Prabhu, 2014). The delivering high-quality care and improved public health were the results of the sustainable health, and care systems. It was easy to imagine a sustainable health and care system, the sustainability of everything that impacted on the health care services such as health promotion, health care instruction, and developing more diversification and sustainable models of health care (Unit, 2020). This showed operation sustainability had a positive relationship with the diversification of health care support activities.

H1.5: There is a positive relationship between the operational sustainability and the diversification of health care support activities of formal MFIs.

2.2. The health care services outreach

The health care services outreach was one of the possibilities to increase access to health services, and better mobilization of health resources to provide health services to the population in remote or underserved areas. The health care services outreach was measured by the number of customers of MFIs (Roodenbeke, 2011). The health care services outreach is associated with all MFIs' operations, it has been regarded as a prerequisite for continuous increasing the diversification of health care support activities and is influenced by many factors, including:

Firstly, number of branches: The distribution, making sure that the products and services was available where and when it was wanted. This included such options such as outreach agents, branches. From the customer's perspective, place referred to convenience and accessibility of the product or service being offered by MFIs. Therefore, the number of branches was one of the factors that positively affected the outreach of MFIs (Churchill and Frankiewicz, 2006). The number of branches was one of the delivery channels for microfinance products and services. Expanding these delivery channels generated convenience and increased accessibility of the product or service being offered by MFIs. At the same time, MFIs were often to improve delivery channels to increase the outreach and thanks to its distribution network such as the branches and transaction points, many MFIs promoted the health care services outreach (Ha, 2020d).

H2.1: There is a positive relationship between the number of branches and the health care services outreach of formal MFIs.

Secondly, productivity: The breadth of outreach was the size or scale of microfinance institutions. The focus on outreach to the customers involved increasing the customer base in MFIs. The staff productivity was significantly positive correlated with microfinance services outreach measure of microfinance institutions. This showed that the productivity had a positive relationship with the health care services outreach of MFIs (Kipesha and Zhang, 2013). The staff productivity positively drove the breadth of outreach of MFIs. The results showed that using the number of customers appeared to be a better predictor of MFIs wider outreach (Abdulai and Tewari, 2017a). Thereby, the productivity had a positive relationship with the health care services outreach of MFIs. The increasing in the productivity resulted into more the number of microfinance customers. The fact that MFIs had higher the productivity that obtained better the breadth and there was the interactive relationship between the MFIs' productivity and breadth of outreach in a positive trend. This showed the MFIs always maintained a combination of the productivity and the health care services outreach, and an appropriate productivity growth strategy contributed to improve the health care services outreach of MFIs (Ha, 2020c).

H2.2: There is a positive relationship between the productivity and the health care services outreach of formal MFIs.

Thirdly, equity growth rate: Equity growth rate contribute to improve the financial capacity of MFIs and financial capacity understood as long-term effects had impact on the microfinance services. Thereby, an improved financial situation was one of the vital factors that contributed to achieving better service diversification, including the health care support services (Hermes, Lensink, and Meesters, 2011). Many MFIs had a low equity and faced many difficulties in attracting the members and customer. Therefore, the less equity growth rate compared to other financial sources, the fewer improvements in the health care services outreach of MFIs (Ha, 2020c).

H2.3: There is a positive relationship between the equity growth rate and the health care services outreach of formal MFIs.

Fourthly, the diversification of health care support activities: The MFIs diversified to offer the services, i.e. product diversification. The results showed that product diversification by MFIs had a positive impact on the outreach. Thereby, this showed the diversification of health care support activities contribute to advance the health care services outreach of MFIs (Nanayakkara and Mia, 2017). Many MFIs diversified to offer the services, i.e. product diversification such as type of different non-financial services offered by formal MFIs. The formal MFIs promoted the diversification of products and services in line with the operation trends and associated with the development strategies, that contribute to increase the outreach of MFIs. In other words, the diversification of health care support activities had a positive impact on the health care services outreach of MFIs (Ha, 2020d).

H2.4: There is a positive relationship between the diversification of health care support activities and the health care services outreach of formal MFIs.

Fifthly, operational sustainability: There was a positive association exists between outreach breadth and sustainability of MFIs. This showed the operational sustainability contributed to expand the services outreach of MFIs (Abdulai and Tewari, 2017b). The operational sustainability had a positive relationship with the outreach breadth of MFIs. Many MFIs increased in operational sustainability and lead to advance the health care services outreach of MFIs (Ha, 2020c).

H2.5: There is a positive relationship between the operational sustainability and the health care services outreach of formal MFIs.

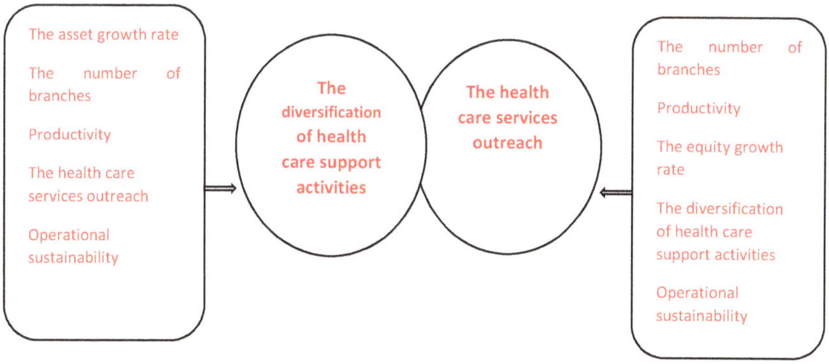

Figure 1. The conceptual framework for the review

Figure 1 summarizes the conceptual framework used, on the conceptual framework basis, in addition to the hypotheses of factors influencing the diversification of health care support activities and the health care services outreach, this study formulates the following two hypotheses that focus on the diversification of health care support activities and the health care services outreach:

Hypothesis 1: There is a positive relationship between the diversification of health care support activities and the health care services outreach of formal MFIs.

Hypothesis 2: There is a positive relationship between the health care services outreach and the diversification of health care support activities of formal MFIs.

3. METHODS

The sources of data are collected from the website of MIX Market, annual reports, financial reports of all formal MFIs in Vietnam from 2012 to 2022. This research has analysed and synthesized the theoretical basis relating to the diversification of health care support activities and the health care services outreach of MFIs. Based on the synthesized and analysed theories, the paper defined the factors affecting the diversification of health care support activities and the health care services outreach, the analysis model of the interaction relationship between the diversification of health care support activities and the health care services outreach of all formal MFIs in Vietnam is established as follows:

$$Y_1 = \alpha_{10} + \alpha_{11}Y_2 + \sum_{k=1}^{n} \beta_{1k}X_{1k} + \mu_1 \quad (1)$$

$$Y_2 = \alpha_{20} + \alpha_{21}Y_1 + \sum_{\gamma=1}^{m} \beta_{2\gamma}X_{2\gamma} + \mu_2 \quad (2)$$

Where,

Y_1 is the variable that measures the diversification of health care support activities, determined by the number of health care support product and service types.

Y_2 is the variable that measures the health care services outreach, determined by the number of active customers. X_{1k}, $X_{2\gamma}$ are the independent variables that can affect the diversification of health care support activities and the health care services outreach in equations (1) and (2), respectively.

The coefficient α and coefficient β are the correlation coefficients of the independent variables with the dependent variables, which are the error terms of the model. For simplicity, indicator i represents the number of observations and indicator t represents the number observed year. This study uses Stata 15.0 software, the definitions of variables and expected signs are presented as can be seen in Table 1.

Table 1. Summary of the research model variables

Variables and symbols	Definition	Data source	Expected sign and hypotheses
Factors affecting the diversification of health care support activities			
Dependent variable			
The diversification of health care support activities (NHT)	The number of health care support product and service types	MIX Market, annual reports, financial reports	
Independent variable			
The asset growth rate (AGR)	Growth in asset	MIX Market, annual reports, financial reports	H1.1: + (high AGR, high NHT)
The number of branches (BRA)	The number of branches	MIX Market, annual reports, financial reports	H1.2: + (high BRA, high NHT)
Productivity: Numbers of customers on numbers of staff ratio (CSR)	Numbers of customers / Number of staff	MIX Market, annual reports, financial reports	H1.3: + (high CSR, high NHT)
The health care services outreach (NAC)	The number of active customers	MIX Market, annual reports, financial reports	H1.4: + (high NAC, high NHT)

Operational sustainability (OSS)	Operating income / (Operating expenses + financing costs + provision for loan losses)	MIX Market, annual reports, financial reports	H1.5: + (high OSS high NHT)
Factors affecting the health care services outreach			
Dependent variable			
The health care services outreach (NAC)	The number of active customers	MIX Market, annual reports, financial reports	
Independent variable			
Number of branches (BRA)	The number of branches	MIX Market, annual reports, financial reports	H2.1: + (high BRA, high NAC)
Productivity: Numbers of customers on numbers of staff ratio (CSR)	Numbers of customers / Numbers of staff	MIX Market, annual reports, financial reports	H2.2: + (high CSR, high NAC)
The equity growth rate (EGR)	Growth in equity	MIX Market, annual reports, financial reports	H2.3: + (high EGR, high NAC)
The diversification of health care support activities (NHT)	The number of health care support product and service types	MIX Market, annual reports, financial reports	H2.4: + (high NHT, high NAC)
Operational sustainability (OSS)	Operating income / (Operating expenses + financing costs + provision for loan losses)	MIX Market, annual reports, financial reports	H2.5: + (high OSS high NAC)

Source: Own study.

This study used regression analysis on a set of panel data, evaluated the fluctuations of variables and performed the correlation analysis. The fixed effects model (FEM) and the random effects model (REM) are the applied models for panel data analysis in this study. The variance inflation factor (VIF) test was carried out on each independent variable of this study model. The research conducted the Hausman test for the model specification for the FEM and REM, and tested for the statistical significance of difference between the coefficients estimates obtained by FEM and by REM, The study chose the result between FEM and REM, and compared them with the pooled ordinary least square model (OLS) to determine the influencing factors for this model and found the impact of the factors on the diversification of health care support activities, and the health care services outreach. At the same time, the study also conducted testing for a variance change to consider the variance change phenomenon, and checked the autocorrelation to examine serial correlation in this model.

4. RESULTS

4.1. Descriptive statistics

This study performed descriptive statistics of both the dependent and the independent variables, which are presented in Table 2. The results found that the AGR, BRA, CSR, NHT, OSS variables had smaller standard deviations than the average, and this indicated that values tend to be close to the mean of the variables. The asset growth rate reduced in some MFIs, due to restructure their operations. The number of branches increased in many MFIs, and 72 branches was the highest. The productivity of MFIs improved over the years, and it achieved over 663 customers per staff. Many MFIs expanded their operations, and the number of health care support product and service types had the highest level of 19 products and services. The operational sustainability always was maintained and improved in many MFIs. The EGR, NAC variables have fluctuations, due to the large difference in the equity growth rate, and the health care services outreach between the MFIs. This indicated that values are spread out over a wider range, and these variables have more variable data in the model. Many MFIs increased the health care services outreach and the equity growth rate every year to meet the needs of members and customers, but some of them reduced the equity growth rate due to restructure their operations.

Table 2. Descriptive statistics

Variable	Mean	Std. Dev.	Min	Max
AGR	23.35575	17.53726	-6.3	69.58
BRA	25.925	22.18383	4	72
CSR	262.3245	175.8024	6.36	663.9
EGR	16.7215	17.43909	-21.1	68.67
NAC	96003.65	108988.8	414	339468
NHT	7.9	5.217328	2	19
OSS	130.5	21.18052	100	178.4

Source: Compiled from data processing results of Stata software

4.2. Correlation analysis

This study tested the multicollinearity, and the multicollinearity occurred when two or more independent variables are highly correlated in the regression model. The multicollinearity test for factors affecting NHT had a result of Mean VIF = 3.25, VIF of variables from 1.10 to 6.25, this result showed no serious multicollinearity in this model. The multicollinearity test for factors affecting NAC had a result of Mean VIF = 3.22, VIF of variables from 1.01 to 6.27.

This result showed no serious multicollinearity in this model.

According to Rule of thumb for interpreting, the size of a correlation coefficient showed that negligible correlation with size of correlation: .00 to .30 (.00 to −.30), low positive (negative) correlation with size of correlation: .30 to .50 (−.30 to −.50), moderate positive (negative) correlation with size of correlation: .50 to .70 (−.50 to −.70) (Hinkle, Wiersma and Jurs, 2003). Accordingly, the analysis results of correlation between variables in the model indicated that the degree of correlation between the variables from negligible correlation to the moderate correlation, so the presence of any multicollinearity was neglected Table 3.

Table 3. Correlation matrix

	NHT	**AGR**	**BRA**	**CSR**	**NAC**	**OSS**
Correlation matrix for factors affecting NHT						
NHT	1.0000					
AGR	-0.1867	1.0000				
BRA	0.5366	-0.0904	1.0000			
CSR	0.5094	0.0649	0.3007	1.0000		
NAC	0.6437	-0.0364	0.4279	0.6574	1.0000	
OSS	0.2675	0.1887	0.2508	0.5718	0.4880	1.0000
Correlation matrix for factors affecting NAC						
	NAC	**BRA**	**CSR**	**EGR**	**NHT**	**OSS**
NAC	1.0000					
BRA	0.4279	1.0000				
CSR	0.6574	0.3007	1.0000			
EGR	0.0668	-0.0048	0.0811	1.0000		
NHT	0.6437	0.5366	0.5094	-0.0056	1.0000	
OSS	0.4880	0.2508	0.5718	0.0645	0.2675	1.0000

Source: Compiled from data processing results of Stata software.

4.3. Regression results

Regression was carried out using FEM and REM, and compared with OLS between the NHT dependent variable and AGR, BRA, CSR, NAC, OSS independent variables. According to the results of FEM and REM, both P-values were less than the significance level of 5% (P-value < 0.001), so the regression models were statistically significant at the significance level of 5 %. In FEM, the variables BRA and NAC had positive impacts on the variable NHT at the significance level of 1% and 1%, respectively; the variables AGR and OSS had positive impact on the variable NHT, the variable CSR had a negative impact on the variable NHT, these variables were not statistically significant. In REM, the variables BRA and NAC had positive impacts on the variable NHT at the significance level of 1% and 1%, respectively; the variables CSR and OSS had negative impact on the variable NHT at the significance level of 10% and 10%, respectively; the variable AGR had a negative impact on the variable NHT, but this last variable was not statistically significant in the model as can be seen in Table 4.

The study examined Lagrange multiplier for REM and FEM, and got results Prob> chibar2 = 1.0000, Prob>chi2 = 0.0000, respectively. The Hausman test was performed to select the appropriate model and the Hausman test result obtained a Pvalue of 0.0692, greater than the significance level of 5 %, so the REM was more suitable than FEM. In comparison to the OLS Pooled model, REM was more suitable than the OLS Pooled model. Therefore, the study used the REM regression results to analyze and test the next steps. Using Breusch and Pagan Lagrangian Multiplier test to examine variance the change of the model, with P-value = 1.0000 was greater than 0.05, therefore, this model did not have the variance change phenomenon. Using Wooldridge test of autocorrelation, with P-value = 0.0232 was smaller than 0.05 so this model did have serial correlation. This study performed to overcome the and serial correlation. The results in REM (xtgls) showed that the variables BRA and NAC had positive impacts on the variable NHT at the significance level of 1% and 1%, respectively; the variables CSR and OSS had negative impact on the variable NHT at the significance level of 5% and 10%, respectively; the variable AGR had a negative impact on the variable NHT, but this last variable was not statistically significant in the model as can be seen in Table 4.

Table 4. Regression results for factors affecting NHT

Independent variables	**Dependent variable (NHT)**		
	FEM	**REM**	**REM (xtgls)**
AGR	0.00613	-0.0167	-0.0100
	(0.43)	(-1.19)	(-0.91)
BRA	0.0979***	0.0960***	0.0949***
	(8.45)	(7.31)	(8.69)
CSR	-0.00998	-0.0119*	-0.0138**
	(-1.81)	(-2.02)	(-3.07)
NAC	0.0000446***	0.0000537***	0.0000549***
	(4.84)	(5.67)	(7.27)
OSS	0.00467	-0.0348*	-0.0242*
	(0.26)	(-2.44)	(-1.97)
_cons	2.945	8.326***	7.146***
	(1.35)	(5.38)	(4.88)
P-value <	0.001	0.001	0.001

Notes: ***, **, * denote significance at the level of 1%, 5% and 10%

Source: Compiled from data processing results of Stata software

In the regression results for factors affecting NAC, the results of FEM and REM, both P-values were less than the significance level of 5% (P-value < 0.001), so the regression models were statistically significant at the significance level of 5 %. In FEM, the variables that had positive relationships with the variable NAC were CSR and NHT, and these variables had significance at 1% and 1% level, respectively; the variable BRA had a negative relationship with the variable NAC at the significance level of 10%; EGR and OSS were not statistically significant variables, although these variables had positive relationships with the variable NAC. In REM, CSR and NHT were statistically significant variables at 1% and 1% respectively, and these variables had positive relationships with the variable NAC; with the significance level of 10%, the variable BRA had a negative relationship with the variable NAC. The last variables had positive relationships with the variable NAC that were EGR and OSS, however these variables were not statistically significant as can be seen in Table 5.

The study examined Lagrange multiplier for REM and FEM, and got results Prob> chibar2 = 1.0000, Prob>chi2 = 0.0000, respectively. The Hausman test was performed to select the appropriate model and the Hausman test result obtained a Pvalue of 0.9175, greater than the significance level of 5 %, so the REM was more suitable than FEM. In comparison to the OLS Pooled model, REM was more suitable than the OLS Pooled model. Therefore, the study used the REM regression results to analyze and test the next steps. Using Breusch and Pagan Lagrangian Multiplier test to examine variance the change of the model with P-value = 1.0000 was greater than 0.05, therefore, this model did not have the variance change phenomenon. Using Wooldridge test of autocorrelation, with P-value = 0.0322 was smaller than 0.05 so this model did have serial correlation. This study performed to overcome the and serial correlation. The results in REM (xtgls) showed that the variables CSR, NHT and OSS had positive relationships with the variable NAC at the significance level of 1%, 1% and 10%, respectively; still at the significance level of 10%, the variable BRA continued to has a negative relationship with the variable NAC; still the variables had positive relationships with the variable NAC, the last variables were not statistically significant that were EGR and OSS as can be seen in Table 5.

Table 5. Regression results for factors affecting NAC

Independent variables	Dependent variable (NAC)		
	FEM	**REM**	**REM (xtgls)**
BRA	-696.6*	-511.7*	-525.3*
	(-2.11)	(-2.01)	(-2.25)
CSR	397.1***	410.2***	406.0***
	(9.05)	(10.96)	(12.15)
EGR	40.06	88.79	81.30
	(0.20)	(0.51)	(0.52)
NHT	10831.2***	9338.2***	9508.1***
	(4.76)	(6.19)	(6.91)
OSS	2.529	78.45	94.22*
	(0.01)	(0.39)	(0.51)
_cons	-76670.2*	-83838.7***	-85586.9***
	(-2.32)	(-3.58)	(-3.97)
P-value <	0.001	0.001	0.001

Notes: ***, **, * denote significance at the level of 1%, 5% and 10%

Source: Compiled from data processing results of Stata software

5. DISCUSSION

The results of REM (xtgls) in Table 4 indicated that variable BRA had a coefficient 0.0949 with the significance level of 1%. As expected, this result was broadly in harmony with the expected sign and hypotheses, and this meant that MFIs focused to expand the number of branches goal was likely to increase the diversification of health care support activities. This meant that MFIs focused to expand the number of branches that were likely to increase the diversification of health care support activities. This helped to diversify the health care support activities for the members and customers, the expansion of more and more the branches and transaction points of MFIs contributed to increase in many the health care products and services, thereby better meeting the health care needs of the members and customers.

The variable CSR had a coefficient -0.0138 with the significance level of 5%. Some MFIs had a high productivity over the years, however they focused on the numbers of customers on numbers of staff ratio to provide some common health care products and services. Therefore, they were not lacked the opportunities to expand the operations for the diversification of health care support activities to meet the needs of diverse customers populations, that included prevention, diagnostics, treatment instruction, nursing care and midwifery, improving the experience of care, improving the health of populations, etc.

The model results showed a very significant impact of NAC on the diversification of health care support activities with a coefficient of 0.0000549 and statistically significant at 1%. As expected, this result was broadly in harmony with the expected sign and hypotheses, and there was a complement relationship exists between the health care services outreach and the diversification of health care support activities. The increase in the health care services outreach contributed to promote the diversification of health care support activities. Beside some common health care products and services, many MFIs met the needs of customers in the health care support activities to achieve the goal of extending as many products and services as possible of MFIs. Thus, the formal MFIs achieved dual goals including the health care services outreach and the diversification of health care support activities over the years.

Operational sustainability has affected the diversification of health care support activities with a negative coefficient of 0.0138 and statistical significance at 10%. Many MFIs have not taken the advantage of operational sustainability to expand operations, providing a wide range of products and services to customers. Beside they met the needs of some common health care products and services, and many MFIs did not meet the needs of customers in the health care support activities to achieve the goal of extending as many products and services as possible of MFIs. This unexpected finding, particularly the trade-off between operational sustainability and diversification of health care support activities showed that operational sustainability was not one of the predisposing conditions to promote the diversification of products and services. The diversification of health care support activities depend on many different factors; increasing in the health care services outreach, allocation of human, material, technical and financial resources to meet the needs of clients will have a positive impact on increasing customer accessibility and expanding more health care services.

The results of REM (xtgls) in Table 5 showed that variable BRA had a coefficient -525.3 with the significance level of 10%. This result was not broadly in harmony with the expected sign and hypotheses, and there was not a complement relationship exists between the number of branches and the health care services outreach. The MFIs' branch was not the only delivery channel for the health care services outreach. Expanding the other delivery channels generated convenience and increased accessibility of the product or service being offered by MFIs. At the same time, MFIs were often to improve the delivery channels to increase the health care services outreach, and thanks to the other distribution networks such as providing online services, contacting households, etc.

The variable CSR had a coefficient 406.0 with the significance level of 1%. This result showed that productivity contributed to improve the health care services outreach. As expected, this result was broadly in harmony with the expected sign and hypotheses. Some MFIs had a high productivity over the years. A high productivity meant that MFIs focused on the numbers of customers on numbers of staff ratio to provide some common health care products and services. Therefore, they lacked the opportunities to improve the health care services outreach to meet the needs of diverse customers populations.

The NHT variable had a positive and very significant impact on on the health care services outreach with the coefficient 9508.1 and statistically significant at 1%. As expected, this result was broadly in harmony with the expected sign and hypotheses, and there was a complement relationship exists between the diversification of health care support activities and the health care services outreach. The increase in the diversification of health care support activities contributed to advance the health care services outreach. Many MFIs diversified the health care support activities to meet the needs of customers in the health care support activities, and they achieved the goal of attracting as many customers as possible of MFIs. Thus, the formal MFIs achieved dual goals including the diversification of health care support activities and the health care services outreach over the years.

There is a significant effect of operational sustainability on the health care services outreach with a positive coefficient of 94.22 and statistical significance at 10%. As expected, this result agreed with the expected sign and hypotheses, and there was a complement relationship exists between the operational sustainability and the health care services outreach. The operational sustainability was one of the suitable conditions to promote the health care services outreach. Many MFIs have taken the advantage of operational sustainability to expand operations, and improving the health care services outreach. They met the needs of customers in the health care support activities to achieve the goal of health care services outreach and attracted as many customers as possible of MFIs.

6. CONCLUSIONS AND RECOMMENDATIONS

Microfinance is seen as a key health care services development tool, and despite the current deepening difficulty within the industry, it continues to grow in Vietnam. The study systematically reviewed the evidence of the impact of factors on diversification of health care support activities and the health care services outreach. This study considered impacts on diversification of health care support activities, and the health care services outreach. The available evidence showed that bidirectional interactions and the causal relationship between the diversification of health care support activities and the health care services outreach.

The study results showed that the two factors that had positive relationships with the diversification of health care support activities were the number of branches and the health care services outreach. The two factors that had negative relationships with the diversification of health care support activities were the productivity and the operational sustainability. The three factors that had positive relationships with the health care services outreach were the productivity, the diversification of health care support activities and the operational sustainability. A factor that had a negative relationship with the health care services outreach was the number of branches. The asset growth rate had an insignificant relationship with the diversification of health care support activities, and the equity growth rate had an insignificant relationship with the health care services outreach. At the same time, this study found relationships between the diversification of health care support activities, and the health care services outreach. The study found a positive bidirectional interactions relationship between the diversification of health care support activities, and the health care services outreach.

The members, customers and poor lack access to the health care services, hence reducing their capability to meet their health requirements. Lack of health care instruction prevents them from maintenance sustainability life. MFIs could be an alternative for the poor to be in a position to meet the demand for health services. They Could benefit the poor's access to health, and need to take an integrated approach to provide a full health care support activities package. This study will help researchers, and managers develop their expertise on key factors of the diversification of health care support activities, and the health care services outreach, and the relationship between the two. Based on the research results, the article recommends the following to increase the diversification of health care support activities, and the health care services outreach:

Firstly, this study found a positive bidirectional causal interaction between the diversification of health care support activities and the health care services outreach, so that the immediate policy recommendation is for MFIs to focus more on the diversification of health care support activities, and the health care services outreach. In order for MFIs to succeed they must promote to maximize health care support activities, and attract more members and customers. At the same time, MFIs should have many combined and synchronous solutions. Because, single solutions continue to be inadequate in confronting the prevalent problems of the diversification of health care support activities, and the health care services outreach.

Secondly, the members, customers and poor need access to a coordinated set of the diversification of health care support activities to have better the health care services outreach. MFIs should take the advantage of operational sustainability to expand the appropriate health care support activities, and they should increase the opportunities to expand the operations for the diversification of health care support activities to meet the needs of diverse customers populations, that included prevention, diagnostics, treatment instruction, nursing care and midwifery, improving the experience of care, improving the health of populations, etc. At the same time, they need appropriate solutions to restrict the trade-off between the operational sustainability and the diversification of health care support activities.

Thirdly, integrated microfinance and health interventions leverage networks of the members, customers and poor to improve livelihoods, promote health care and safeguard against highly cost illnesses. Non-integration of the diversification of health care support activities, and the health care services outreach can be highlighted as a limitation factor to the health care support-promoting capacity of the MFIs' operations in Vietnam. Therefore, MFIs should expand the other delivery channels generated convenience and increased accessibility of the health care support activities being offered by MFIs. MFIs need to improve the delivery channels to increase the health care services outreach, and thanks to the other distribution networks such as providing online services, contacting households, etc.

Fourthly, the diversification of health care support activities were to be integrated on a massive scale with microfinance services for the members, customers and poor, then the true potential of microfinance to improve the health care services outreach and offer a dignified route out of care could be realized. Thereby, the policies and strategies of MFIs should facilitate and enforce integration of health care support activities and health education components into their designs to maximize their health care support-promoting capacity.

References

Abdulai, A. and Tewari, D.D. (2017a). Trade-off between outreach and sustainability of microfinance institutions: Evidence from sub-Saharan Africa. *Enterprise development and microfinance*, 28(3), 162-181.

Abdulai, A. and Tewari, D.D. (2017b). Determinants of microfinance outreach in Sub-Saharan Africa: A panel approach. *Acta Commercii*, 17(1), 1-10.

Churchill, C.F. and Frankiewicz, C. (2006). *Making microfinance work: Managing for improved performance*. International Labour Organization.

Hà Văn Dương (2020a). *Tài chính vi mô: Các chỉ số đánh giá và mối quan hệ tương tác*. Việt Nam: Nhà xuất bản Kinh tế Thành phố Hồ Chí Minh.

Hà Văn Dương (2020b). *Tài chính vi mô: Mô hình hoạt động và định lượng*. Việt Nam: Nhà xuất bản Kinh tế Thành phố Hồ Chí Minh.

Ha, V.D. (2020a). *Microfinance: The Assess indicators and Interactive Relationship*. Ho Chi Minh City Economic Publishing House.

Ha, V.D. (2020b). The Interactive Relationship Between the Credit Size and Financial Sustainability of The Formal Microfinance Institutions in Vietnam. *International Conference on Contemporary Issues in Finance, Banking and Accounting for Sustainable Development*. Hanoi, Vietnam, Vietnam National University of Economics and Business: Science and Technics Publishing House.

Ha, V.D., (2020c). *The Interactive Relationships in Microfinance*. Chisinau, Republic of Moldova, Europe: Eliva Press.

Ha, V.D. (2020d). *Impact Measurement of Microfinance Outreach*. Chisinau, Republic of Moldova, Europe: Publishing house: Eliva Press.

Hermes, N., Lensink, R., and Meesters, A. (2011). Outreach and efficiency of microfinance institutions. World development, 39(6), 938-948.

Hinkle, D.E., Wiersma, W., and SJurs, G. (2003). *Applied statistics for the behavioral sciences*. Houghton Mifflin College Division.

Hubbard, R.G. (2007). *Money, the financial system, and the economy, 6th Edition*. United States: Addison-Wesley Reading, MA.

Kent, D. and Dacin, M.T. (2013). Bankers at the gate: Microfinance and the high cost of borrowed logics. *Journal of Business Venturing*, 28(6), 759-773.

Kipesha, E.F. and Zhang, X. (2013). Sustainability, profitability and outreach tradeoffs: evidences from microfinance institutions in East Africa. *European Journal of Business and Management*, 5(8), 136–148.

Leatherman, S., et al. (2012). Integrating microfinance and health strategies: examining the evidence to inform policy and practice. *Health policy and planning*, 27(2), 85-101.

Leatherman, S. and Dunford C. (2010). Linking health to microfinance to reduce poverty. *Bulletin of the World Health Organization*, 88, 470-471.

Nanayakkara, G. and Mia, L. (2017). Does product diversification and emphasis on profitability in microfinancing alleviate poverty? *Asia-Pacific Development Journal*, 23(1), 21-56.

Primiana, I., Masyita, D., and Febrian, E., (2018). Social outreach model and efficiency in Sharia micro finance institution: literature review. *European Research Studies Journal*, 21(3), 104-122.

Rashid, A. and Twaha, K. (2013). Exploring the determinants of the productivity of Indian microfinance institutions. Theoretical and Applied Economics, 18(12), 83-96.

Rao, K.R.M. and Fitamo, T.L. (2015) Concepts and Measures of Outreach and Sustainability in Microfinance Institutions (A Comprehensive Literature Review). *International Journal of Science and Research* (IJSR), 4(2).

Rauf, S.A. and Mahmood, T. (2009). Growth and performance of microfinance in Pakistan. *Pakistan economic and social review*. 99-122.

Roodenbeke, E.D. (2011). *Outreach services as a strategy to increase access to health workers in remote and rural areas*. World Health Organization.

Quayes, S. (2012). Depth of outreach and financial sustainability of microfinance institutions. *Applied Economics*, 44(26), 3421-3433.

UNESCAP (2007). *Microfinance for Poverty Reduction: Building Inclusive Financial Sectors in Asia and the Pacific*. Development Papers No 27. Manufacture in Thailand: United Nations.

Unit, S.D. (2020). *What is Sustainable Health? Microfinance for Poverty Reduction: Building Inclusive Financial Sectors in Asia and the Pacific*. Available from: https://www.sduhealth.org.uk/policy-strategy/what-is-sustainable health.aspx.

Zeller, M. and R.L. Meyer (2002). *The triangle of microfinance: Financial sustainability, outreach, and impact*. Washington, D.C: International Food Policy Research Institute.

Schreiner, M. (2002). Aspects of outreach: A framework for discussion of the social benefits of microfinance. *Journal of international development*, 14(5), 591-603.

Sim, J. and Prabhu, V.V. (2014). The Sustainability and Outreach of Microfinance Institutions. *IFIP International Conference on Advances in Production Management Systems*. Springer.

Srinivasan, G. (2013). *Microfinance India: The social performance report*. SAGE Publications India.

www.ingramcontent.com/pod-product-compliance
Lightning Source LLC
LaVergne TN
LVHW022314200926
848481LV00004B/1338